BETTY HAHN

STEVE YATES

Essays by

DAVID HABERSTICH
AND DANA ASBURY

Catalogue by

MICHELE M. PENHALL

University of New Mexico Press, Albuquerque
Museum of Fine Arts, Museum of New Mexico, Santa Fe

BETTY HAHN

PHOTOGRAPHY OR MAYBE NOT

FIRST EDITION
Library of Congress Cataloging in Publication Data
Yates, Steven A.
Betty Hahn: photography or maybe not / Steve Yates;
essays by David Haberstich and Dana Asbury;
catalogue by Michele M. Penhall.
—1st ed.
p. cm.
Includes bibliographical references.
ISBN 0-8263-1601-8. — ISBN 0-8263-1602-6 (pbk.)
1. Photographic criticism. 2. Photography, Artistic.
3. Hahn, Betty, 1940–   .
I. Haberstich, David.   II. Asbury, Dana.
III. Penhall, Michele M.   IV. Title.
TR187.Y38   1995
770'.1—DC20   95-4358
                                    CIP

FRONTISPIECE (PP. III-IV): *details from* Hoofbeats,
from the series B Westerns, *1993, photolithograph
with applied Van Dykes, monotype, and pencil,
25 x 36.*

CONTENTS

Acknowledgments VIII

Late Modern, Postmodern, and After:
The Photographic Pluralism of Betty Hahn
Steve Yates 3

The Early Years
David Haberstich 13

Riding the Range:
The Straight Photographs of Betty Hahn
Dana Asbury 39

Plates 60

The Photographic Work of Betty Hahn, 1964–94
Michele M. Penhall

ILLUSTRATED CHRONOLOGY 172
CATALOGUE OF WORKS 178
COLLECTIONS 192
SELECTED EXHIBITION HISTORY 194
SELECTED BIBLIOGRAPHY 197

ACKNOWLEDGMENTS

A BOOK OF THIS COMPLEXITY COULD NOT HAVE BEEN put together without the generous assistance and support of caring people who worked beyond expectations. We owe an enormous debt of gratitude to the late Roberta DeGolyer who began the work of interviewing and cataloging with great enthusiasm, understanding, and humor. She carefully recorded detailed information, and this groundwork provides a scholarly resource here and at the Museum of Fine Arts.

Special thanks to David Haberstich, senior curator of photography at the National Museum of American History, Smithsonian Institution, who traveled across the country to gather research for his personal historical essay. Dana Asbury provided remarkable assistance as an essayist and supporting editor. Historian Michele Penhall spent incalculable hours organizing and completing the Catalogue of Works, making it into a concise research tool for the future. Becky Schnelker, curator of Tamarind Institute at the University of New Mexico, offered helpful guidance to the catalogue format and information as did the International Museum of Photography at George Eastman House, other institutions, and private collectors.

To designer Kristina Kachele and the University of New Mexico Press staff who put these ideas and works into their present visual form, we offer our continuing respect and thanks. Further appreciation goes to Karen Fabricius who assisted the curator and artist in every aspect of the publication and exhibitions, to Alan Labb who photographed each work for this book, and to Georgia Smith who designed the artist's catalogue system.

This publication originated with the traveling exhibition, funded by the National Endowment for the Arts, which opened at the Museum of Fine Arts, Museum of New Mexico, Santa Fe. We appreciate the efforts of Cindy Graves, Helen McCarty, and Christie Schooley of TREX (Traveling Exhibitions Program at the Museum of New Mexico), and the support of the Jane Reese Williams Committee of the New Mexico Council on Photography and the museum's Photogroup as well as the administrative staffs within the Museum of New Mexico. We express special thanks to director of the Museum of Fine Arts David Turner and secretaries Theresa Garcia and Wilma Casias-Schofield, registrar Joan Tafoya, preparator Charles Sloan, and exhibition designer Nancy Allen and her staff.

Our gratitude to Lynne Yates, Charles McClelland, Andrew Smith, and friends who provided encouragement each step of the way.

STEVE YATES AND BETTY HAHN

BETTY HAHN

Detail, Bracketed Exposure, *from* The Wasted Film Trilogy,
1972, gum bichromate on fabric with quilting, 45 x 14.

LATE MODERN, POSTMODERN, AND AFTER

The Photographic Pluralism of Betty Hahn

STEVE YATES

The medium is as unimportant as I myself.
Only the forming is essential.
KURT SCHWITTERS

The artist's work is to be measured
by the vitality, the invention, and
the definiteness and conviction of
purpose within its own medium.
MAN RAY

SINCE THE MIDDLE OF THE TWENTIETH CENTURY, artists using photography have pursued many directions outside the conventional modes of medium. The autonomy of individual art forms, as defined by Clement Greenberg in his treatise "Modernist Painting," has become less important to artistic discourse.[1] Meaning, genres, styles, and standards unique to each art medium no longer forge the paths in this era of contemporary art-without-category.

Increasingly, artists are inventing unlimited forms of expression in the photographic milieu, and historians are relying less on the definition of mediums or the fundamental tenets of modernism, as put forth by Greenberg, to evaluate this pivotal era. In addition, the multifaceted work of artists such as Betty Hahn has set the stage for endeavors outside the art movements of the twentieth century.

Such transformations have occurred at critical junctures throughout world history, as in the early 1900s, during the dawn of modernism, when new practices began to redefine the artistic canon. At the same time, photography was emerging as a medium, establishing its own vernacular, thanks to independent breakthroughs by Alvin Langdon Coburn, Pierre Dubreuil, Paul Strand, Charles Sheeler, and others working in the currents of progressive art. These artists, as well as critics who reviewed their work, pioneered a self-sufficient language for photography and claimed for it a primary role alongside modern painting, architecture, sculpture, music, and literature.[2]

Their breakthroughs provide a striking parallel to work by contemporary innovators. Artists of both eras stepped

(left) 1. Pierre Dubreuil, Interpreta-
tions Picasso: The Railway, *c. 1911,
photogravure. Collection of the
Museum of Fine Arts, Museum of
New Mexico, gift of Tom Jacobson.*

(right) 2. Paul Strand, The White
Fence (Port Kent, New York),
*1916, gelatin silver photograph.
Collection of the Museum of Fine
Arts, Museum of New Mexico, gift
of Michael Hoffman. Copyright
Aperture Foundation.*

including music. By 1909 Coburn and Dubreuil were paral-
leling the Cubists and the Futurists (Fig. 1).

Only a few years after making his first semiabstract still-
life photographs in the spirit of Cézanne's work, Strand
defined the purpose and nature of the modernist approach:
"Photography . . . finds its *raison d'être*, like all media, in a
complete uniqueness of means. . . . The full potential power
of every medium is dependent on the purity of its use."[3] His
doctrine was best exemplified by pictures that reduced objects of everyday life to pure form, such as a white picket
fence against an unfocused field of grass and geometric
facades (Fig. 2).

beyond tradition, combining aspects of existing styles with
unconventional approaches, and thereby creating progressive alternatives to accepted doctrine. Early modern photographers began by using elements of pictorialism, modern
urban subjects, and tenets of form found in the other arts,

stract expressionism, with unconventional photographic dimensions (Fig. 3). Modernism became a potential resource for contemporary artists—much as pictorialism had for the early photographic modernists—out of which to develop nontraditional approaches with historical relevance. But, where the early modernists forged a distinct model for photography by concentrating on its inherent qualities, contemporary artists such as Betty Hahn have used many sources, both inside and outside photography, to discover qualities and relationships determined by something other than the unique characteristics of a single medium, genre, category, or style.

Thus, photographic art by Hahn, Rauschenberg, and others has evolved without the descriptive label of a movement. No one approach, style, or medium has predominated. These unconventional photographic artists appropriated preexisting artwork and photographs along with images from nonartistic sources, subjects, and materials. Unlike the modernists, these contemporary artists do not seek to create the signature masterpiece or archetypal image. While assimilating various modern and postmodern aspects into their work, they continue to evolve by adding new photographic forms of expression to the mainstream.

Few artists are able to sustain inventive prerogatives that transcend historic periods of change. Betty Hahn's diverse contributions tell us a great deal about the nature of late-twentieth-century art that does not depend on tradition.

In 1964 Hahn began to explore an uncharted territory

Half a century later Greenberg fully articulated the modern premise, placing it in a historical context that spoke to a new generation of artists. At the same time, in order to break with the past, Robert Rauschenberg and other artists began to combine modern modes of expression, such as ab-of ideas between mediums. Instead of seeking to define a single medium, process, approach, or style, she continues to develop her ideas through a variety of photographic inventions. Conceptually, her work transcends traditional materials and linear formulas. It defies the categorization of late modernism as it expands the possibilities of photographic expression.

Hahn establishes patterns of ideas as ongoing forms of discovery, reversing the modern paradigm of reduction and archetype into an open-ended model of variations. Repetition, a key characteristic of photography, lies at the heart of such discovery. It is an important tool with seemingly unlimited potential. In the course of this repetition, Hahn regenerates ideas in many directions: untested thoughts interact with each other to broaden photographic possibilities with fluid points of view. The artist takes part in a process of assimilation, rather than one of reduction or distillation.

During the 1960s Hahn was determined to move from the static refinement of black-and-white photography into other experiences. In an early statement of intent she found even the notion of visual expression too limiting: "I prefer a visual occurrence to visual expression . . . to unify a variety of elements into the visual production of my ideas."[4] This approach is the antithesis of Greenberg's codification and Strand's view of a "complete uniqueness of means" whose power "is dependent on the purity of its use." On Hahn's workbench of ideas nothing ever remains the same.

One of her first major works to engage this approach is *Wasted Film Trilogy: 1,000 Dusty Negatives, Bracketed*

Exposure, and *Strip of Six* (Plates 103–5). Re-creating, on a large scale, part of a strip of film of impromptu portraits made at a photographers' party in New York City, this study in negative and positive forms denies historical conventions in photography.[5] The works in this triptych, related only marginally through the re-created sprocket holes running alongside the repeated images, include disparate materials with little relationship to portraiture or any modern standard of purity. *Wasted Film Trilogy* stands as a manifesto against traditional approaches to photography, indeed breaking with all modern forms of expression.

However, this watershed piece also makes reference to several ideas from the waste heap of photographic aesthetics, leading to the essential underlying ideas Hahn pursues outside conventions. These fundamental ideas are represented by the sections of this book: the *repetition* and *variation* of images rather than the production of a single fine print; the diversification and *ambiguity of space* replacing the single viewpoint, or "window-and-mirror" references, of the photograph; the incorporation of color as an independent expressive element in black-and-white photography; the pursuit of the *anomaly* as the final form of expression rather than as an accident for disposal; and the development of *cinematic and narrative sequences*. These themes constantly influence Hahn, both consciously and unconsciously, forming a working matrix from which arise prospects beyond categorization.

In establishing a styleless mode of photographic production, Hahn, like Rauschenberg, helped lay the foundation for practices by contemporaries such as Sigmar Polke, Anselm Kiefer, and Christian Boltanski. Unlike the modernists, these artists, with their disparate modes of photographic innovation, remain happily outside any collective tradition, aesthetic direction, shared method, or master's lineage.

Traditional photographers decry such experimentation as ephemeral, a digression from existing conventions, or, at best, as a temporary lesson. Twentieth-century masters often attempted departures from existing practices, but usually within their own proven style or manner. These innovative practices have generally been excluded from the stylistic and thematic divisions of history. Critics have depicted them as peripheral, transitional, a temporary use of mediums and materials based on trial and error, and in the service of some "greater" end.

In a rare response to like charges, Picasso clarified the difference between thoughtless invention, and meaningful and lasting innovation: "I have never made trials or experiments. Whenever I had something to say I have said it in a manner in which I have felt it ought to be said. Different motives inevitably require different methods of expression."[6] Over the last three decades Hahn has used a variety of methods springing from many motives; however, she does know how to exploit the essence of what is gained through the risks of experimentation. Her work is a prolific source for understanding the pluralism that characterizes the art of the 1990s.

During the early twentieth century, artists such as Hannah Höch explored new forms of photographic expres-

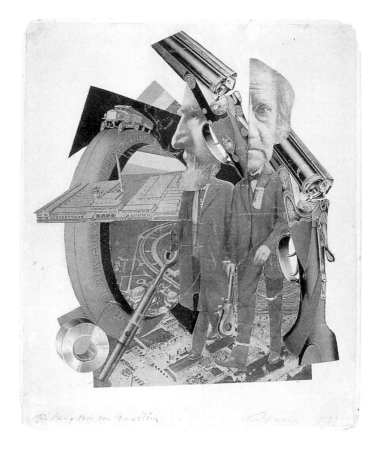

4. *Hannah Höch*, High Finance, *1924, photomontage. Courtesy of Galerie Berinson, Berlin.*

sion in a parallel manner. Höch helped invent photomontage without using a camera (Fig. 4). Unorthodox in approach, she assembled pictures found in magazines, newspapers, and books rather than create original prints in the darkroom. Defying formal art principles, she appropriated the vernacular of everyday imagery, much as Hahn later did in her series *Who Was That Masked Man?* (also known as

The Lone Ranger series). Höch's genius, however, lay in the editing and arrangement of chosen elements and in the character of their raw-cut edges. Sustaining a life of their own, her photomontages reflect a new concept of space like a fragmented, animated stage, moving from the realism of photography into the domain of culture.[7]

Like Höch, Hahn is a prolific investigator of existing sources as well as unconventional avenues. She has repeatedly used the Lone Ranger—an American icon whose image she appropriated from an anonymous Hollywood studio portrait found on a greeting card—in variations exploring numerous ideas and materials, from drawings with different

photographic mediums to ceramic plates. Her flexibility of purpose cannot be satisfied within a single medium, and late modern or postmodern criteria are ineffective in fully assessing the value of her pluralistic devices. She develops her ideas through various photographic and nonphotographic means using a process that only partially relies on what the camera records.

Hahn shares with Höch a passion for the contrasts and contradictions of culture found in Dada photomontage. However, Hahn's pieces maintain their own problems and solutions. She has learned how to harness chance and experimentation in the course of pursuing visual innovation.

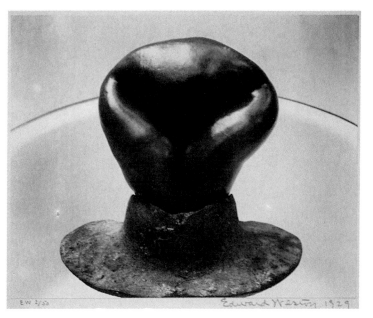

(opposite) 5. Late-nineteenth-century family portrait, photomontage. Collection of Betty Hahn.

(left) 6. Edgar Degas, La famille Bellelli. *Postcard from the collection of Betty Hahn of a painting in the Musée d'Orsay, Paris.*

(right) 7. Edward Weston, Pepper and Bone, *1929, unique gelatin silver photograph. Collection of Michael Mattis and Judith Hochburg.*

The artist also tampers with the myth that photographs can only provide reliable forms of objective reality. Often her work paradoxically assures veracity even as it questions the truth-bearing capacity of the camera. From her stitched fabric photographs to her highly descriptive details of flower arrangements, veracity coexists with many other possible forms of meaning. This underlying ambiguity enriches the possibilities for interplay with the viewer. Hahn invests every work with multiple dimensions of meaning. The medium is not the message but a springboard to epiphanies on the nature of reality.

Ironically, traditions and images inside and outside photographic and art history do serve a catalytic role in Hahn's inventive strategies. From the beginning, the work of anonymous photographers has been as valuable to her as that of Edgar Degas, Edward Weston, or Piet Mondrian (Figs. 5–8). Anomalous nineteenth-century photographs made on various materials provide striking parallels to Hahn's early stitched gum prints (Figs. 9, 10). However, her use of such sources attests to more than appropriation, postmodern issues, or historical influences. It acknowledges her true motives in making what Picasso distinguished as lasting innovative alternatives to artistic rules or idioms. Hahn's contributions undermine the artificial separation of photography

(left) 8. Piet Mondrian, Flower, *1908, pencil drawing. Collection of Béla T. and Edna Kalman.*

(top right) 9. Artist unknown, Untitled (windmill), *c. 1890, silver photograph on silk. Helmut Gernsheim Photography Collection, Harry Ransom Humanities Research Center, University of Texas at Austin.*

(bottom right) 10. Artist unknown, Explanatory Drawing to Accompany the Instructions for Firing Abel's Torpedo Primer, *late nineteenth century, diagram on photosensitized cloth. Helmut Gernsheim Photography Collection, Harry Ransom Humanities Research Center, University of Texas at Austin.*

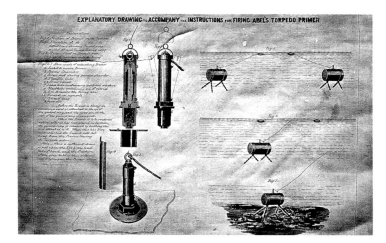

from other art forms. She pours the perceptions gained in her unrelenting investigations directly into the crucible of all visual art.

Hahn's work transforms perception, informing the new pluralism with an unorthodox relevancy. She challenges the viewer's understanding of a photograph as a piece of reality like a memory. The diverse contributions of Betty Hahn are a necessary prerequisite to the appreciation of contemporary art, which continues to refuse categorical distinction and to proliferate in direction as we enter the next century.

NOTES

1. "Each art had to determine, through the operations peculiar to itself, the effects peculiar and exclusive to itself. . . . It quickly emerged that the unique and proper area of competence of each art coincided with all that was unique to the nature of its medium . . . each art would be rendered 'pure,' and in its 'purity' find the guarantee of its standards of quality as well as of its independence" ("Modernist Painting," *Art and Literature* 4 [Spring 1965]: 193–201).

2. For a historical framework of early modern photography, see Steve Yates, "Proto Modern Photography: The Artist and the Critic," *Proto Modern Photography* (Santa Fe: Museum of Fine Arts, Museum of New Mexico, 1992).

3. Paul Strand, "Photography," *Camera Work* 49–50 (June 1917): 3; *Seven Arts* (August 1917): 524.

4. Artist's statement, June 1969, n.p., collection of the artist.

5. These multimedia portraits of collector and dealer Lee Witkin and other photographers were made at a party organized by critic A. D. Coleman and portrait photographer Neal Slavin. About *Wasted Film Trilogy*, see the Catalogue of Works in the back of this publication.

6. Marius de Zayas, "Picasso Speaks," The Arts (May 1923); reprinted in Goldwater and Treves, eds., *Artists on Art from the XIV to the XX Century* (New York: Pantheon, 1945; 3rd ed., 1972), 417–18.

7. For an analysis of this transformation from the actuality of the photograph into the cognitive space of culture in Dada photomontage, see Stephen Foster, "The Cognition of Culture: Berlin Dada, Photography and the Ideology of Space," in Steve Yates, ed., *Poetics of Space* (Albuquerque: University of New Mexico Press, 1995).

BETTY HAHN

The Early Years

DAVID HABERSTICH

SOME OF BETTY HAHN'S COLLEAGUES WHO HAVE known her for a long time, myself included,[1] always felt that she was up to something, with her enigmatic, mischievous Giaconda smile, which could unnerve and make you suspect that she was laughing at you. Something of this comes across in her self-portrait as an angel, superimposed on a late, deckled-edge cabinet print from the Hoffman studio of Thorntown, Indiana.[2] Indeed, her work is suffused with gentle mischief, disarming and faintly mocking. For someone predisposed to a fine sense of humor and irony, both her training and chosen medium could hardly fail to sharpen her wit. I suggest that wit is precisely the common factor which unifies this artist's oeuvre, from her earliest successes to her most recent, regardless of ostensible style, method, or subject, but the pleasures of viewing this artist's work extend far beyond humor.

THE EDUCATION OF AN ARTIST

Hahn's initial artistic experiences involved painting and drawing, later graphic design. She did not take photography seriously at first—which is not unusual for many of its most ardent devotees—but it helps explain her flexibility. If she was a beneficiary of the playful spirit of the 1960s, conversely, she should be regarded as one of the authors of the plot to make serious art fun.[3] While the turbulent spirit of the period is well known and documented, not everyone

(opposite) Detail, Red Building, *1973, 9 x 13 gum bichromate on 16 x 20 fabric with stitching.*

wishes to recall the extremes of savagery which accompanied the Aquarian Age, and which persist in some of the hard rock and rap music of the 1990s. If the young were at times encouraged by the Jerry Rubins to murder their parents, some did so metaphorically or symbolically in their art. But Betty Hahn never produced a vicious work of art. Her art has always been subversive, but it is a visual and cerebral subversion, accomplished through a light touch and charm. The 1960s were a baroque period for the arts, when stoned hippies, enterprising commercial illustrators and promoters, and committed artists alike experimented with combinations of media. Betty Hahn was a part of this ambiance and interchange, beginning with her student days at Indiana University.

Hahn was profoundly influenced by the imagery of Robert Rauschenberg (whose assemblages she saw after she had begun making woodcuts), Andy Warhol, and others who combined photography with the traditional processes of printmakers, painters, and sculptors. The work of Warhol in the early 1960s relied heavily on the appropriation of cultural icons and mass media imagery, and similar themes, as well as formalistic similarities, are found in some of Betty Hahn's *later* work. But Warhol and Rauschenberg[4] came from painting traditions (and, in Warhol's case, advertising illustration), whereas Betty Hahn was one of the first to bring specifically *photographic* training, traditions, critical theory, and sensibilities to multiple-media works, arguably the first *important photographer* who emerged from the 1960s to question photographic convention by successfully combining photography with other media. Initially attracted to art through drawing, painting, and design, a fortuitous exposure to Henry Holmes Smith convinced her that photography was serious, potent stuff, and she eventually settled into the comfortable but exciting dialogue with photography which would characterize her career. Hahn's work is self-referential, both in terms of personal biography and in the sense of probing the history of a medium which had become a significant part of her life: it is largely about the medium of photography, even when utilizing nonphotographic means to comment upon it, whereas Warhol selected photographs to signify, embody, and disseminate aspects of popular culture. When Hahn appropriates images from published sources, as in the extensive Lone Ranger series, she is most like Warhol. Warhol became an art superstar—famous, notorious, and popular, in part, because popularity was his subject, and everyone is fascinated with the impact and mechanism of fame, however much they may claim to deplore it as vapid, meaningless, or corrosive. Hahn's art is not as popular, collectible (or expensive) as Warhol's, in part, because her work is more arcane, more specialized, as well as more (that is, too) supple and subtle. I disagree, however, with Jonathan Green's assertion that "nonsilver printmakers never learned what Warhol and Rauschenberg knew so well: that one had to juxtapose, not merge, the differences between media"; that "[they] reduced the possibilities of form and expression to mannerist techniques"; or that they overindulged in their media frenzy without solving fundamental artistic problems. These are sweeping generalizations which cannot logically be applied to all nonsilver printmakers or all multiple-media pieces, and Green's premise—that one must juxtapose rather than merge media —is flawed. Although presumably he intended to be descriptive rather than prescriptive, the result is pedantic and reminiscent of Helmut Gernsheim's rules for acceptable photographs.[5]

Hahn's work is usually *about* photography, regardless of the disparate media employed (Fig. 11). It is seldom specifically *about* popular culture, even when it explores the use of photography to circulate cultural ideas and icons. The accessibility of a Warhol or Rauschenberg, in contrast to the distance engendered by the bewilderment and antagonism felt by the uninitiated toward, say, Abstract Expressionism or Surrealism, is largely due to the general viewer's comparative ease in relating to either the jokes or the tragedies of popular culture embedded in their work, owing to a familiar iconography. Much of Hahn's work is circumscribed by the philosophical and technical issues and traditions of photography; it requires more training and specialization to comprehend. For example, she employs inside jokes, understood only by the cognoscenti of photography; she addresses a more specialized audience in the same sense that Oriental painting can be fully understood and appreciated by a comparatively small public.

Not only is Betty Hahn's temperament gentler than that of many male painters of the period, but her humor is usually subtler. The darker, more biting humor of even a close photographic colleague like Robert Fichter was not to her

11. Kodak Tri-X Pan Film, *1968,* gum bichromate on paper, 22 1/2 x 15.

taste. Her references to, or illustrations of, the epistemological and semiological problems of photography (as well as its nuts, bolts, and tools) automatically limit her audience. This tendency has much to do with her relationship with her "only" real teacher of photography, Henry Holmes Smith.

An almost linear genealogy extends from one generation of teachers to the next, from László Moholy-Nagy to Henry Holmes Smith to Betty Hahn, to her students, some of whom undoubtedly are teaching in art schools as well. That a lively Betty Hahn gum print may appear to share little stylistic ground with an enigmatic Moholy-Nagy photogram or semi-abstraction does not nullify this spiritual connection. Moholy-Nagy and Henry Smith, who met in 1937, had no need to practice or defend traditional documentary photography, for the utility of photography as a faithful witness had long since been proven and accepted, and the aesthetic pleasures of pure photographic textures, surfaces, and forms were well known. Their questioning and enlargement of photographic convention concerned what *else* photographic vision and photographic techniques could do —what was their expressive potential?—and this quest resonates through their teaching and finds its most complete realization in the work of Betty Hahn. The richness of the modernist creative tradition of Moholy-Nagy through Henry Holmes Smith is confirmed by the results: a second generation of influential masters with such widely varying styles, subjects, and messages, as Hahn, Jack Welpott, Robert Fichter, Jerry Uelsmann, and Jaromir Stephany.

These artists and others who could be cited were liberated by Smith from the limited photographic ideology promulgated by didactic historians like Gernsheim, whose primary works tend to view nondocumentary approaches as "experimental" cul- de-sacs or aberrations, misguided, sometimes morally indefensible, diversions of the inexorable destiny of the photographic mainstream.[6]

Hahn and Fichter epitomize one mode of reaction or refraction through the Smith filter, while Uelsmann represents another logical manifestation. Welpott's most well-known imagery fits comfortably within the unmanipulated "standard" by which most photographic images are measured, whereas the abstract "cosmological" meditations of Jaromir Stephany most closely resemble Smith's own cliché-verre prints, both in method and result. Yet all these diverse styles rely fundamentally upon the power of the automatic, unmanipulated photographic image as a reference point. Uelsmann's multiple-image montages form a world of fantasy, dream, myth, and personal allegory through a photographic gateway—a synthesis of René Magritte paintings, Joseph Cornell boxes, and Val Telberg photomontages, achieved through purely photographic techniques—which astound and fascinate precisely due to their distinctly photographic appearance. They always look authentically, seamlessly photographic, however unlikely or bizarre the combination of optically convincing elements or fragments.

Hahn and Fichter opted for the handmade look of prints and paintings and imposed extra-photographic methods upon a photographic base. Whereas some of Fichter's work employs photography primarily as a tool, there is a beauty and unity in Hahn's work that renders it a satisfying, multifaceted, intricately interconnected exposition of photography, its traditions, its role in our lives, and its sometimes surprising affinities with other arts. More than any other artist, in my mind she summarizes, recapitulates, almost embodies, the history of photography. Those half-hearted, belated attempts to squeeze photography into introductory art historical texts such as Janson's *History of Art*[7] fail because they neither come to grips with the distinctive tradition of photographic image-making required to provide a structure to explain the unique accomplishment of a Betty Hahn nor integrate it into the larger artistic and intellectual milieu. Her work may remain part of this separate history of photography until critics and historians can evolve some broad new history of the visual arts capable of analyzing nontraditional forms of photography as readily as it can accommodate deviant painting and sculpture.

THE YEARS WITH HENRY HOLMES SMITH, ARTIST, PHILOSOPHER, VOLATILE PEDAGOGUE[8]

After having been invited by Moholy-Nagy to teach at the short-lived New Bauhaus in 1937 (Moholy was impressed by Smith's color experimentation), Smith wrote for the leading amateur photographic magazine of the period, *Minicam Photography,* and became associate editor in 1939–40. Although he wrote articles on "creative" and "experimental"

techniques such as solarization,[9] which helped introduce Moholy-Nagy's ideas to amateur photography, they could not satisfy his restless temperament for long. Smith's dye-transfer prints from cameraless cliché-verre negatives, as well as his long admiration for the camera "abstractions" of Aaron Siskind, form an obvious link to Moholy and Bauhaus teachings, but have little obvious stylistic connection with Hahn's work, other than their inspiration to solve artistic problems via photographic means. One tenet of modernism is that the exploration of a technique or medium for its expressive potential can itself constitute a sufficient artistic problem. The essential element which Moholy-Nagy, Smith, and Hahn shared was the compulsion to break down aesthetic and philosophical barriers.

Invention, innovation, and exploration have characterized Hahn's work in its many forms and guises. Never content to work within the confines of a tradition or genre, she has consistently sought to extend boundaries or break them, to blur the lines between photography and printmaking, photography and painting, the single and the multiple image, the decisive moment and the extended narrative, craft and art, the comic and the serious—not as experimentation for its own sake, but to find the most appropriate means of expression for her sensibility, and to force the issue, force the evolution of her art. Her work seeks both an explication and a resolution of dichotomies, of seemingly incompatible methodologies, and even of documentary evidence vs. invention, the automatic recording of a machine vs. the craftsman's hand and the artist's intellect. The early classic painted and/or stitched gum-bichromate snapshots which brought her to prominence clearly announced her bold enterprise and, characteristically enough, were at once powerful and audacious, yet soft and modest.

In photography the sixties were a "decade of renaissance during which photography emerged as an academic discipline. An ever-expanding network of university programs supplied personnel for museums, galleries, and more college classrooms."[10] Henry Smith's classroom had long been one of the isolated outposts which made the advancement of photography on these fronts possible in the late 1960s, and, ultimately, validated these trends with dollars through the acceptance of photographs as collectible commodities.

Betty Hahn was poised to embrace the creative efflorescence of the sixties, impatiently waiting for it to begin. After spending the summer of 1963 in New York, she concluded that its photographic life was still so consumed by photojournalism that there was actually more happening photographically in Henry Smith's Indiana. Besides Smith, her design teacher, George Sadek, and graphic arts professor Rudy Pozzatti were influential, and the Indiana art historians also had a strong impact on her vision and analytical techniques for discourse about art. Clearly there are strong threads of both an academic understanding of art historical processes and issues, as well as a reverence and even nostalgia for the past, which are woven into the fabric of her work (not only her work on fabric, if one can excuse the facile pun). Betty's most important colleague was fellow graduate student Robert Fichter, whose attitude and humor

helped emancipate her from a ponderous approach to history. She was "too serious" then, she admits, aiming to be another Harry Callahan or Henry Cartier-Bresson. Fichter was at once respectful, yet irreverent, toward Beaumont Newhall's canon of photographers and images, and helped her to pass quickly through the typical artistic adolescence of emulating popular, famous artists. They teased, but encouraged and supported each other. She influenced him with her gum printing in 1965, inspiring him to make the connection with printmaking which would characterize and animate his work.

She sometimes regrets having had only one teacher of photography, and would like to have studied with someone like Minor White also.[11] She would have found that White had much in common with Smith, for their years of correspondence and collaboration in workshops, *Aperture* articles, and other projects marked them as kindred spirits who were each energized by the other's intellect and passion for photography. As impressive as White was as a lecturer and as great a force as he has been in photography, Smith is often considered the better teacher because his students were less imitative. White's students at the Rochester Institute of Technology recognized this tendency by deriding colleagues for producing "Minorgrams," work thought to resemble superficially his presumed style. Although Uelsmann, who studied first with White, then Smith, exhibits the influence of both, his style probably owes a greater debt to both Smith's historicism and his liberating inspiration.

At the risk of seeming unduly autobiographical and anecdotal, I offer a few personal recollections about Betty Hahn and Henry Holmes Smith to illustrate her relationship with him. My involvement with Betty and Henry was neither unique nor especially significant at this time, but I was a fly on the wall during portions of Betty's early career. In 1963–64 I observed the interaction between Smith and Hahn while an art history graduate student in the Department of Fine Arts at Indiana University (Bloomington). Former Smith student Jaromir Stephany, then at the George Eastman House, had alerted Henry to my arrival in Bloomington, where I was to inherit the slide-making assistantship established by Stephany for the department's slide library —an appropriate symbol of a transition from photographer to art historian. A grinning Minor White had prophesied that, since Henry Smith had put Stephany on his feet but I was already on mine, he would probably turn me on my head. Indeed he did, for no one was ever quite the same after a dose of Henry's potent medicine.

I used Henry's darkroom facilities to process black-and-white slides, considering myself a pioneer, following in the footsteps of photographer-turned-art-historian Peter Bunnell,[12] a warrior in the battle to ensure photography's legitimate niche in art criticism and scholarship. I assumed Henry would welcome me as an ally, but instead he was gruff and distant, for he thought I was a photographic apostate rather than a fellow crusader. As I assessed the politics of this predicament, he seemed to display a double inferiority complex. Art historians ran the department and seemed to have little interest in the studio faculty, and the lone pho-

tographer was a pariah among these artists, isolated and misunderstood, or worse—peripheral and ignored. Such assumptions about the department paralleled an analysis of the Rochester Institute of Technology's School of Photography, which during that period was dominated by the photographic science faculty, while the art or "illustration" faction sometimes felt itself ignored or unfavored. Years later, Betty would find herself in circumstances at R.I.T. resembling Henry's at Indiana, although for different reasons. Henry, in any event, saw me not as an ally but another enemy on his ever-lengthening list.

I once observed Henry apparently being intimidated by his patrician, authoritarian department chairman, Henry Radford Hope, while he unpacked an acquisition of Edward Weston prints for the university art museum—he seemed to be having a difficult time justifying the photographs to the baleful Hope eye. It was an almost mythical scene—the beleaguered photographic apologist[13] passionately but ineptly trying to enlighten the academic snob. Additional evidence of Hope's condescension toward Smith surfaced in a meeting of Ph.D. candidates in Hope's home, as the chairman suggested asking Smith to teach the art history faculty and graduate students how to make lecture slides from book illustrations and to photograph archaeological fragments. He considered art historians a breed of super-scholars who effortlessly accumulated skills as required by their research —if your study led you to Urdu sources, for example, you would pause and learn Urdu, and if your work required photographic skills, you would take a short course with your local neighborhood photographic technician—for example, Henry Smith. But Hope temporarily demurred in a patronizing manner: "But perhaps not—the poor man [Smith] has been so busy and beside himself lately, I worry about his health. Maybe we should table the idea."[14]

In the second semester I registered for Smith's graduate seminar in the history of photography because I wanted to write a Ph.D. dissertation in the history of photography with Henry as my major advisor. At registration, the art history graduate student who signed me up snidely muttered, "I didn't know they gave credit for that course," neatly summarizing and substantiating Smith's uphill struggle. Perhaps Indiana University was a comparatively receptive place for a photographer to incorporate the history of photography within a traditional fine arts curriculum, but it would not be easy.

So I found myself in Henry's classroom with Betty, Robert, and a few others in that heady spring of 1964. The intimacy of the format, as expected, produced a different dynamic than a lecture class with Beaumont Newhall, but it was also startlingly different from studying with Newhall on a one-to-one basis. The seminar was a rich introduction to the philosophy of Henry Smith and his deep dissatisfaction with the existing histories of photography. He demanded consideration of neglected photographers and critical evaluations of their contributions to the medium, and asked us to produce our own lists of the "fifty greatest" photographers; a wide variety of responses would ensure lively debate. When one student included the name of Henry

Holmes Smith, Henry publicly scorned the blatant apple-polishing but privately purred. New concepts, such as photographs as "residues" of reality, energized discussion. Students were asked to describe what a photograph "should look like" and to formulate constructs upon which photographers could be measured and new critical histories could be spun out. John Crowley's response, that a photograph should look like "the tension between reality and artifice," seemed a profound concept with which to appraise the unique and mysterious potency of photographic imagery in its many guises, and which informs the art of Smith and many of his varied students—quintessentially, Betty Hahn. Despite the surly registrar's disdain and the chairman's apathy, Henry's course was a paradigm for all art historical inquiry.

A minor incident illuminates Henry's and Betty's personalities. One rainy day when a short paper for the seminar was due, I lacked a protective envelope or briefcase and was concerned that an illegible, soggy paper might blur the clarity of my thoughts. Since Henry seemed lenient about deadlines, I gambled on a late delivery, but he was livid that I had not brought the paper to class and was unimpressed by my excuse. Betty suddenly said, "And my dog ate my paper." Devastated by the resulting laughter, I soon realized that Henry's anger had subsided, that her quick wit had defused the situation and probably protected my grade. This charming little gesture, the timely recycling of a moribund old joke, prefigured Betty's penchant for reusing, reinventing, recombining, and reinvigorating creaky clichés of art and craftsmanship into brilliant new forms and statements. She knew how to handle both her materials and her professors.

Through the seminar, Henry gradually realized that I was no traitor after all, but my new fear was that he might extend his paranoia to me. He confided that the art history faculty intended to sabotage my graduate school career and invited me to transfer into his M.F.A. studio photography major. Disappointed and feeling that Henry wasn't taking *me* seriously, I wanted to think it over and decided to take a year off before resuming my academic career. Eventually, after finding a museum job, I drifted into another university and never returned to Bloomington. I have daydreamed that I did, however, either (a) to rejoin the struggle, on that particular front, to convince scholars of photography's legitimacy, Smith in his way and I in mine; or (b) that I capitulated and took an M.F.A. with Henry, forming a famous triumvirate with Betty and Robert Fichter—I might have been part of their "movement."

Betty had been a student at Indiana University since her freshman days in 1958. Henry was her undergraduate advisor and she was in a sense apprenticed to him for eight years—all of which she needed, she believes, to assimilate what he said. He was eccentric but brilliant, and his passion for photography stimulated and exhilarated. His classroom/studio was a technical and intellectual laboratory in which ideas were tested and weighed, and this certainly is exemplified in Hahn's conception of her work. He advocated "reading" photographs,[15] but when not contemplating or reading

photographs, or exulting in the medium, he was being irritated by a myriad of distractions and annoyances which made him "sore." He yelled and vented his passions lustily, occasionally resorting to minor physical mayhem. His wife, Wanda Lee, verified that life with him was punctuated by a series of "explosions."[16]

Smith was a frustrated, insecure, artist/philosopher/teacher, a workaholic with an ambivalent, love/hate relationship with the teaching profession. He loved it, but seemed powerless to prevent it from consuming him. In her long association with Smith, this lesson was not lost on Hahn, that he gave much to his students, then hated them for taking it; that he lavished time on freshmen, too shallow, immature, and inexperienced to appreciate his brilliance, then threw tantrums if they failed to be dazzled. Yet, as Hahn ruefully points out, he designed those decisions for himself. She had to beg to be allowed to help him free himself for his creative work. She assumed that her job included housekeeping chores in addition to the teaching and more glamourous activities, so she pitched in, trying to dissuade him from obsessively cleaning darkroom sinks by himself. He had set himself a routine which many college professors and most artists would find inimical to the creative process, spending five full days and several evenings per week in the Fine Arts Department, although he could have spent two of those days in his studio instead of frittering them away on interruptions. I consulted him when the department's copy camera broke down, but instead of simply advising me, he insisted on packing and shipping the camera himself, noisily bustling about while sarcastically complaining; during this uproar, I resolved to avoid being the occasion of his future martyrdom or inconvenience.

At times, Henry seemed manic-depressive, alternating violent explosions with an elfin affability and humor. His face was usually red, either with mirth or anger. Constantly in motion, he would hum and giggle, dropping outrageous witticisms along his path, then become instantly enraged if provoked. A Jerry Uelsmann double-portrait montage of himself and Henry depicts him in a typical posture: arms folded, resembling Jack Benny stifling a laugh, his cheeks rosy with delight. A sequence of photographs of him with Beaumont Newhall at a symposium shows him collapsing in hilarity.[17]

Henry taught Betty partly by indirection and bad example, and she had his flaws, such as his inability to control his schedule, "burned into her memory": she vowed not to fall into the same trap of frustration and procrastination. Teaching has "taken its toll" on her, but she has never allowed it to dominate her. Smith, hungering for recognition that either never came or came too late, neglected his children as well as his art, Hahn notes—while students—*other* people's demanding children—probably received his fatherly attention. Hahn determined to be neither demanding child nor irritant. A keen observer of the Smith drama, she never fought him or indulged in ego conflicts. Rather, she learned from his wit and wisdom, philosophical insights, penetrating inquiries, practical experience, and technical expertise. She resolved to be a helper and facilitator,

straightened his office and cleaned his darkroom, as if these tasks were integral to the internship process. Through her long association with him, clearly she apprenticed herself to him in the old-fashioned, time-honored manner of craftsmen, almost conjuring up visions of Renaissance ateliers. Under the tutelage of this tortured, quirky master photographer/craftsman/ thinker, Hahn learned to emulate and appreciate his best, to reject counterproductive excesses, to establish dominion over both her materials and her schedule, and to blossom into a creative but pragmatic, methodical, albeit whimsical, force, a playfully serious artist and a well-adjusted human being. Her eight years of exposure to the many facets of Henry Holmes Smith helped to produce a consummate artist.

If she sometimes wishes that she had had additional photography teachers for greater breadth, students of multiple teachers nevertheless may envy the depth of her personal chemistry with Smith. Undoubtedly Betty also had an influence on Henry which provided him with salutary effects; she must have served as a counterbalance to the annoyances with which he afflicted himself. Perhaps the flurry of activity late in his life, completing old projects, participating in more exhibitions, was partly a response to Betty's success and even a stimulus to a spirit of competition. Her extensive Lone Ranger series, dating from 1974 to 1978, is reminiscent of the many variations of Smith's "Mother and Son" images (even in terms of the double-figure form), forty-two of which were shown in his 1973 retrospective at Indiana.[18] Some free association about the Smith and Hahn series suggests provocative links between the two myths, the two projects, and the two artists—for example, "Mother and Son" (or father and daughter?); the Lone Ranger and Tonto (Henry and Betty?). Certainly Betty played Tonto to Henry's Lone Ranger before galloping off into her own private sunset.

It seems axiomatic that Smith would benefit from his more mature students and their discoveries. Hahn's direct encouragement and participation, as well, undoubtedly, as her personal example of enthusiasm, industry, and determination in seeing her own projects through to completion ultimately made his retrospective exhibition possible. A provocateur like Robert Fichter may have offered as much aggravation as reward (Smith's smoldering pique when Fichter mischievously announced that he planned to change his graduate major to anthropology is another vivid memory of the Bloomington days), but Betty gently smoothed his ruffled feathers whenever possible. She continues to express her gratitude to him for everything he taught her, and accepted the predictable disappointment that he never quite reciprocated. His letters to her are restrained, but his admiration and grudging gratitude can be detected between the lines.

Years later, when Hahn tried to tell Smith how much he had meant to her, he growled, "You got everything from Fichter." He was embarrassed by the sentiment, she assumes, yet she understands his jealousy of Fichter's influence. She protested, but triangles involving famous teachers and their famous students must be among the more complex human relationships to analyze or endure. The high intensity of passions in fields like the arts constitute high risk factors when teachers and students have made heavy investments of emotion, talent, and careers in each other. Once, when Smith saw Hahn's published pictures accompanied by a biographical statement, he was angered and hurt to see that his name and her special relationship to him had been edited out and subsumed into a stark citation of her Indiana University degree, whereas her short workshop with Nathan Lyons was prominently mentioned. Since she had spent eight years working side by side with Smith but only about ten evenings in Lyons's class, naming Lyons but not Smith was disproportionate and misleading. For the sake of historical accuracy as well as self-preservation, she took pains to circumvent further wounded feelings by exerting tighter control over her future biographical statements.

Proportion and perspective, indeed, are as crucial in biography as in figurative art. It is wrong to place undue emphasis on Smith's failures, notorious temper, and fragile ego: more than a bundle of volcanic bluster or wounded feelings on one hand, or elfin charm on the other, he was truly a central figure in twentieth-century photographic art as pedagogue, artist, critic, theorist, and agitator. To describe his personal idiosyncracies is to posit them as factors in the development of Betty Hahn's personality, art, and teaching style. She certainly *didn't* get "it all" from Robert Fichter— she undeniably got most of it from Henry Holmes Smith. The questions he asked about photography were hers also, but her means to respond and test his ideas, as well as the ability to formulate her own questions and answers, she developed at his elbow. That a superior teacher begets superior students scarcely needs elaboration or proof, but as part of this process, students (or children) often experience growth via rebellion and reaction against their teachers (or parents).

ROCHESTER: ROBERT AND ALICE

After receiving their Master of Fine Arts degrees in 1966, Robert Fichter, and later Betty Hahn, moved to Rochester, New York. At first Betty photographed in New York City, and, although armed with her M.F.A., the usual prerequisite for college art teachers, she was not initially drawn to the academic world. Despite her experiences with the vigorous, questioning philosophy and personal experimentation of her mentor and the exuberance of her own creative output as a graduate student, she was willing to sacrifice that freedom to the hard economic realities of the workaday world. She applied for many jobs which would have utilized her technical skills as a darkroom technician, printer, or "straight" documentary photographer. Mildly interested in advertising as an outlet for her design training, she found it disappointing and looked elsewhere. In Ithaca she spent a few months making art history slides for Cornell University, then moved to Rochester, where she continued unsuccessfully to seek photographic employment with Kodak, Xerox, and other

firms, ultimately settling for an unrelated job as a social worker for two years.

Fichter had taken a position at the International Museum of Photography at George Eastman House, where he discovered the photographs of Atget, Bruguière, and Moholy-Nagy, reinforcing his interest in the expressive potential of nonpurist photography. He also discovered there Alice Andrews, a fellow employee and photographer who had studied with Nathan Lyons. Alice Wells and her three children had been living with Daniel Andrews, a Kodak engineer, for some years, and in spring 1962 she had taken his surname, although they never actually married.[19] Robert became intrigued with her double-frame prints, while she became hopelessly intrigued with him.

Betty and Alice individually found intellectual and artistic stimulation in the work and personality of Robert, but they would be linked through their romantic relationships with Daniel Andrews, whom Betty later married. Betty acknowledges no particular artistic interaction with Alice, although Alice had generously loaned her darkroom to Betty. But the interrelationships among Betty, Robert, Alice, and Daniel obviously were rich and complex.

Betty considered Alice more of a "pure" or "documentary" photographer than she was, but this does not accurately describe Alice's approach. Betty, Alice, and Robert, as well as colleagues like Tom Barrow and Roger Mertin, also in Rochester at that time, shared that quintessentially sixties attitude in photography which challenged the rules of fine-print photography.[20] Even if Nathan Lyons had a greater impact on Alice than on Betty, Betty could not fail to notice the correspondence between his "constant" question— "What do you mean by 'photographic?'"—with Henry Holmes Smith's line of inquiry, "What should a photograph look like?" Betty and Alice were each stimulated by a charismatic teaching artist who initiated fertile dialogues about their medium. Lyons lectured on "vernacular" and "snapshot" photography to workshop students like Betty, Roger Mertin, and Alice,[21] reinforcing Betty's interest in this "folk" tradition. If Alice preferred standard, mass-produced photographic materials and was not as interested or as adept in hand-coated photography as Betty, there are nevertheless affinities of form and intention. Betty, Alice, and Robert all developed multiple-image works, for example, and Alice's major series of pictures, *Found Moments Transformed,* based on a collection of anonymous, old negatives brought to her by Fichter, amply indicates shared concerns.

Teaching photography was one of the few remaining viable career choices that would utilize Betty's university training. At first she applied for a position in the School of Photography at Rochester Institute of Technology, but relates that the chairman, William Shoemaker, turned her down on grounds that he had never hired a woman to teach.[22] Betty remembers him asking, "How would it look to have a woman in the darkroom with all those boys?" Having known the jolly, witty Shoemaker for four years, I was puzzled when Betty related this incident. Small cadres

of women students had integrated the R.I.T. darkrooms and studios many years earlier; putting a few women students in the dark with boys never seemed to bother anyone. The sexism of the early sixties among male students revolved chiefly around the jokes that women (a) attended technical colleges primarily to earn an "M.R.S." degree, and (b) studied photography if they were not attractive enough to be glamour models (they were sometimes called "Schultzy" in dubious honor of the plain, wisecracking photographer's assistant in Robert Cummings's television sitcom). The high school joke about taking a girl into the darkroom "to see what develops" was already passé; mixing the sexes in the rather public R.I.T. darkroom complex was simply not an issue.

But equal educational opportunity does not ensure equal employment policies. No one can condone bias, overt or covert, or hiring misconduct, but Shoemaker's students think he was capable of tossing off an outrageous excuse or reviving a hoary joke to solve a knotty problem, such as whether to hire an inexperienced instructor who made unconventional pictures. In those still benighted times stereotyping was so ingrained that it could be invoked to excuse inaction. Without programs to promote gender equity, a perception of bigotry might seem safer than risking a damaged ego, admitting ignorance, or annoying a conservative faculty. Shoemaker, a photographic scientist with predictably conservative views on art, may have had more prejudice toward Betty's pictures than her sex. This is conjecture, not history, but 1960s avant-garde photography was not always welcomed by the photographic establishment, and when the innovator was a woman, issues could be complex: Hahn may forget how radical her work looked. The school had recently exported its most controversial, enigmatic image-maker, Minor White, to the Massachusetts Institute of Technology. White's abstract formalism and mystical, contemplative approach to photography were not universally appreciated, and his preoccupations and introverted personality scarcely fitted him for a good-old-boys' club— but at least he made "straight" silver prints. Still a vivid memory, although having departed years earlier, was the flamboyant Ralph Hattersley, an outspoken maverick and "beatnik" who had refused to embrace the clubby atmosphere of the faculty rooms and had scandalized some professors by marching students in mock military style to local bars for classes. A conservative defensiveness among long-term professors with long memories would not be a surprising reaction to an application from a young woman who might have proved to be another "difficult" artist and whose multimedia prints were hard to understand. Perhaps Shoemaker's question, "How would it look to have a woman in the darkroom with all those boys?" really meant, "How would you feel as the only woman in a group of good old boys—or crotchety old men?"[23] Eventually Hahn thwarted Shoemaker, whatever his motive, when she found employment with another R.I.T. college, the National Technical Institute for the Deaf. When Tom Muir Wilson became head of the School of Photography illustration pro-

gram, he managed to get Betty transferred, and she taught there for seven years.

Her position at R.I.T. essentially replaced Minor White's fourth-year program. She was ill at ease there indeed, partly because she found the seniors a great challenge and always felt an outsider on the faculty, never accepted or treated as an equal, even when joined by a female colleague, Judith Steinhauser. This isolation was exacerbated by the antipathy of female students, who refused to study with a woman. Forced to confront this issue, she realized that she had no female role models in photography. Although she doesn't believe women have an inherently different sensibility than men,[24] and her work at times has offended feminists, she and most women in the arts eventually have had to give serious consideration to the relationship between their work and their status as women. That she chose to go against the grain and ally herself proudly with stereotypically "feminine" crafts like needlework is a testament to a woman who has always had the courage to think for herself and allow her art to unfold without deference to prevailing winds (notwithstanding a surprising affinity with the feminist artist Judy Chicago's concept of "feminine crafts" vis-à-vis the organization of her "dinner party" project). When pressed, she cited as female role models Agatha Christie, Georgia O'Keeffe, and Ingrid Bergman,[25] and although Agatha Christie inspired her parodies and explorations of crime, forensic, and surveillance photographs, these "role models" otherwise seem to function in only the most general sense—unless Bergman's portrayal of Joan of Arc, a courageous feminine leader of men, had any specific resonance.

Through Van Deren Coke, who had been director of George Eastman House from 1971 to 1972, she found a teaching position at the University of New Mexico, which was actively seeking a woman artist. Betty and New Mexico were eminently suited to each other, so Albuquerque became her permanent home and base of operations. There she has flourished as an artist and a teacher, and has sought to make these distinct roles compatible with each other, rather than to be torn between them. She has tried to be as open, lenient, and nonjudgmental about image-making as Smith had been, but feels that she is more structured and tougher in terms of requirements and assignments, which helps to protect her own creative life.

EXHIBITING BETTY'S WORK

As a curator of photography at the Smithsonian Institution it was my job to be aware of new currents in photography, so when I saw Betty's work in the late 1960s, I resolved to exhibit it. The Division of Photographic History had embarked on what we thought was an important series of exhibitions of the work of women photographers. Beginning with an Imogen Cunningham retrospective, it ran to four separate exhibitions[26] before the idea was abandoned

as photographers increasingly expressed doubts (or annoyance) about participating in such a series. They rightly had qualms about being identified as "women" photographers, and wanted to be regarded simply as "photographers." Perhaps the series smacked of exploitation for curatorial mileage, but Betty had expressed no reservations and was paired with Gayle Smalley in the second show.[27] Her work was refreshing and new, yet with delightful photo-historical and photo-technical references. There were multiple levels of playful perversity in details such as the giant, hand-colored 35mm sprocket holes which appeared in her gum-bichromate prints. The contrary concepts of allowing this modern photographic symbol or identifier to appear, heroically enlarged, in the medium which so many photographers had attempted to use to simulate paintings, then applying bright painted accents to the holes, was intellectually provocative, tastefully irreverent, and amusing. By comparison, the work of Gayle Smalley had less impact, but the exhibition demonstrated the liveliness of new uses for tired old media, as well as how different the work of two artists could be, even when both used photographic means and essentially the same sub-genre. Time and again Betty's prints have outshone seemingly similar work in group exhibitions.[28]

The modest opening reception was a bit strange, for both Betty and Gayle seemed subdued and oddly remote. Resplendent in a large, broad-brimmed hat, Betty had an air of mystery. She looked stunned or dazed, although her parents were proudly beaming. Perhaps she was disconcerted

(left) 12. Betty, Passport Photo,
1970, 14 x 10 3/4 silver gum
bichromate with black stitching
on 20 x 16 fabric.

(right) 13. Dan, Passport Photo,
1970, 14 x 10 3/4 silver gum
bichromate with brown stitching
on 20 x 16 fabric.

to hear her own voice hovering above, repeatedly describing how Henry Smith had encouraged her to try gum printing, for included in each exhibition of this series was a taped interview with the artist. The show was a hit, although there were no reviews, negative or positive; Washington newspapers seldom reviewed photographic exhibitions in those days. It was not Betty's first exhibition, but reviews or not, I believe it was pivotal: perhaps her reflective mood signified her recognition of that fact.

Her work was included in later Smithsonian group exhibits, such as a portrait exhibition, "The Camera and the Human Facade" (1970),[29] whose avowed purposes were not only to provoke dialogue about portraiture (see Figs. 12, 13), but to display and delineate as much diversity of form, color, style, texture, and psychological approach as photography could offer a single subject category. Later Betty's prints from the History of Photography Collection were contrasted with older, pretentious, painterly gumbichromate prints in a group exhibition, "New Images 1839–1973" (1973), which compared early photographs utilizing "obsolete" processes and twentieth-century "revivals." Naturally, the work of Betty Hahn was prominently featured, and in fact had inspired the show and stimulated the increased collecting of contemporary work by "alternative" processes. The multiple-gum, romantic, imitation paintings of Charles Booz and others contrasted sharply with Betty's exuberant, brilliantly hued prints, some with those enlarged 35mm sprocket holes and film edge imprints which proclaimed that her work had photographic origins

and avoided hackneyed examples of the post-Pictorialist notion that all evidence of photographic techniques should be camouflaged before a photograph was aesthetically acceptable. Although all the prints in the two-woman show had been on paper, Betty donated for this show some of her newer work on fabric, a technique which would occupy her from 1970 to 1973. The 1960s had ended, and she had already launched a new phase of creative exploration based on this early work.

INTO THE SEVENTIES AND BEYOND[30]

The work of Betty Hahn is often self-referential and biographical, as in her commemorative stamp series, and is frequently rooted in the snapshot idiom. But the exploration of this tradition is not an exclusive commitment, for she is fascinated by many other media issues, including the traditions of fine-art photography and the icons of professional photography. For example, in 1971 she made Rolleiflex negatives of fruits and vegetables "á la Weston" (her phrase) but tried to replicate the colors of the real objects with gumbichromate pigments—a technical tour-de-force. In contact printing twelve #120 rollfilm negatives together, she alluded to the utilitarian look of a professional photographic object which many amateur snapshooters have never seen—the contact sheet. She was chided for this "attack" on Edward Weston, but in actuality it functions partly as homage, not blasphemy, acknowledging his pre-eminence as still-life

14. Lettuce, 1972, 10 3/4 x 13 1/2 green gum bichromate with green stitching on 16 x 20 fabric.

with her own, still firmly grounded in photographic practice and history (Fig. 14).

The fabric photographs alluded to another photographic tradition of the turn of the century, when family photographs and other images of sentimental value were being printed in cyanotype and other processes on silk, cotton, and linen for application to decorative, utilitarian objects. The result was to expand and redefine the boundaries of photography, and to introduce textures and colors impossible with standard photographic surfaces. Betty's cloth photographs also employed private and sentimental imagery in direct reference to this nearly forgotten aspect of our combined photographic and cultural heritages. "I think a lot of my stuff is sentimental," she said. "Nowhere . . . is a stranger, they're all my friends." Her husband, friends, and favorite objects all inhabit these works.[31]

Also in 1971, she began looking for details in her photographs that resembled stitching. She was self-consciously seeking "empty," "folk-y" imagery, but previsualized stitched elements to enliven what she calls the vacancies in literal photographs, especially those deliberately produced within the limited technical means of amateurs. She liked the "perversity" of manipulating passport photographs—breaking the rigid, precise State Department rules. Much of her stitching was not fancy but minimalist, and could be seen as referring to the tradition of stitchery rather than attempting a virtuoso performance. She transformed stitchery and made it substitute for characteristics or elements of photographs, describing how light-colored stitching func-

photographer while lampooning the notion of any patented, exclusive approach to the genre. Despite its multiple layers of meaning, this work constitutes one of Betty's simpler statements—it offers an alternative to Weston's vegetable imagery, quietly matching the master's technical virtuosity

tions as "highlight retrieval" for images with inadequate tonal separation. To stretch a metaphor like a thread, she was performing surgery with a needle on ailing photographs. She sees much of photography as a folk art, for "everybody's snapshots look alike," so it was logical to combine it with other folk arts. Thus, in this apparent contradiction, Hahn even plays brilliantly with the technical limitations which distinguish vernacular photographs from professional images made by experienced photographic craftsmen who seek the fullscale/full substance ideal which must be squeezed out of the medium, for photography, with all its promise of effortless simulations of reality, does not always yield such replication without a fight. This is another aspect of the tension between reality and artifice which Henry Smith's students were taught to recognize. Hahn, despite being herself thoroughly versed in all the tricks of the photographic artisan, substituted and celebrated the tradition of another folk medium to rescue a technically flawed photograph. More than a clever commentary on craft traditions, this method simultaneously merges media, revitalizes and re-examines the myth of photography, and creates objects of gentle, provocative beauty. Not the least of the messages of these pictures is the power of intelligent parody (Fig. 15).

Betty grasped the genius of early American samplers, this quintessential "woman's" art, so the anonymous women of the American crafts tradition, as well as the snapshooters who casually chronicled family history, became her missing female role models. The insistence on process in her work

and "humourous references to art history serve the contemporary desire for intellectual games in art." Her "fundamental innocence—a refusal to be difficult"[32] remains a hallmark of her work. Her embroidered gum prints were "fearlessly decorative," according to Van Deren Coke.[33]

15. Bristol Garden, 1973, 9 x 13 green gum bichromate with white, blue, and purple French knots on 16 x 20 tan fabric.

There were photographic jokes in series such as *Bracketed Exposure* and *1000 Dusty Negatives,* as well as connections with Pop art, repetition, and machines.

"Hahn's work has a frontier vitality and unpredictability that is not unlike the eclectic energy that animates Albuquerque's urban character," suggested one critic.[34] Elsewhere, Steve Yates questions the notion of eclecticism, preferring the word *heterogeneous.*[35] After all, in blending two media, what she did was not fundamentally different from a painter's use of two different colors, applied with two different types of brushes, to produce two contrasting areas of a composition. Hahn's work is unpredictable merely because she operates so intuitively. If that notion, which admittedly requires an unconventional leap of the imagination, can be accepted, perhaps we can allow that Hahn is simply an artist with a very large palette. Purist photographers who bristle at hearing their pristine silver prints accidentally called "paintings" by well-meaning exhibition designers might do well to recall that Fox Talbot's metaphor about "drawing with the pencil of nature" is the point of departure for most of the official histories of photography. If Hahn's work frequently invokes those hermetic histories and specialized traditions, it nevertheless embraces many other visual traditions and provides more than mere ironic juxtaposition, more than warmed-over dadaist and surrealist gesture, more than eclecticism—it integrates, unifies, and equalizes disparate materials, means, and contexts.

Hahn readily acknowledges her debt to traditional folk arts—especially those of women—and has expressed her emotional connections to the needle arts. Indeed, she sees much of photography as a folk art.[36] Yet, despite the innocence critics have cited, her years of training and exposure to Smith provide a sophisticated understanding of her process and results, and their complex relationships to multiple aesthetic traditions. "Responding to the possibilities of the 'new' process was, for me, like changing from a simple declarative sentence, however carefully rendered, to a compound, complex statement of fact and fantasy. The picture was no longer synonymous with the subject because I could manipulate the process. . . ."[37]

Her crime photographs, by contrast, were a complete departure, a return to straight photography. They were influenced by the famous *Incredible Stack o' Wheats Murders* series by Les Krims,[38] and related to her interest in mystery stories, but she later pronounced the whole episode a faux pas. These pictures were never exhibited and she is a bit embarrassed by them, but it was a necessary step for her to take. "Straight" photography can be so loaded, charged, beyond the artist's control, she was reminded, that she had to return to manipulated photography, literally to regain emotional and aesthetic control. This inability to control pure or straight photography does not refer to the technical niceties of exposure, density, contrast, but to the ultimate interpretation of a work as a function of viewer response—to the result of the reductive, documentary power which we have learned to associate with and ascribe to images with the clues which signify "straight photography." Whether categorized broadly as "straight" or "manipulated," or con-

sidered in terms of the differences between minute variations of process, subprocess, subject, genre, and dozens of
other facets, photography is to Betty Hahn a "huge cafeteria" (or a huge palette, depending upon one's orientation as
consumer or creator) of attitudes, processes, and materials
—a rich, adventurous mix of possibilities. Far from being a
tortured artist, she has been having fun exploring all these
possibilities all these years, honing her intuitive powers, and
at the same time her discoveries have substantially enriched
the expressive vocabulary of photographers and other
artists.

REVERIE

It is May 1993 when I finally find myself in Betty's pleasant
studio, pondering the shimmering residue of her life's work.
I review the early gum prints, renewing acquaintances with
old friends as if at a class reunion, and move on to the newer pieces, many of which I confess I have never seen before.
I pause when a recognizable face appears—here a Robert,
there an infrequent Alice. Henry's letters and published
writings, the books and articles about him, have been
moved aside. But his spirit lingers. How is it possible that
twenty-nine years have elapsed since Betty and I were in his
classroom together? Betty has discreetly disappeared, leav-
ing me alone with her quiet, efficient assistant, who carefully pulls prints from map drawers, replacing others we have

finished admiring. We murmur uncritically that we like this
one or that one especially—we like them all, really—una-
bashed responses that, oddly, seem to say and mean everything. They're all flat works because Betty hasn't ventured
into the realm of sculpture and installation pieces (yet) that
the current avant-garde uses to explore "affective" photography, which largely means photography as subject.[39]

The Albuquerque spring has been gorgeous, as Betty
promised. I visited the city only once before, to see Van
Deren Coke and Tom Barrow in 1974, just a few weeks
before Nancy Newhall's untimely death (if only I had had
time to go to Santa Fe), and prior to Betty's departure from
Rochester. Now I've returned to Albuquerque a few months
after Beaumont's death. Betty has changed and so have I,
yet we're the same in many ways. In the initial telephone
conversation to arrange my visit, our first direct contact in
uncounted years except for a couple of letters, she remarked
that it seemed as if we had talked only the other day, that
nothing had altered. That was how I had felt about the letters. But photography has changed: Betty's vast cafeteria of
processes, techniques, modes, and ideas has expanded. How
many new recipes will find their way into her repertoire?
Her proverbial plate is pretty full already. Most of the new
photographic avant-garde seems too cerebral to translate
well into another artist's art. But if anyone is capable of
looking at other artists looking at photographs, it's Betty
Hahn. And how much of the new art is even conceivable
without the stimulus of the Henry Smiths, Nathan Lyonses,
Robert Fichters, and Betty Hahns of the 1960s and 1970s?

A fine and fruitful legacy, I am thinking as the last of Betty Hahn's Hahns are returned to their drawers.

I always knew that Betty was up to something.

NOTES

1. I have known Betty Hahn through intermittent glimpses over a span of nearly thirty years, and I have usually been slightly suspicious of her and uneasy in her presence. It may surprise her to know that. Or perhaps not. Perhaps she was merely responding uncertainly to some discomfort she felt in my presence because I was confused and introverted when I met her. In any case, this opportunity to reconsider Betty and her work has produced some miracles of understanding that make a project like this enormously rewarding. I know her better now and have acquired new insights.

2. Reproduced in the exhibition catalog *Into the Seventies: Photographic Images by Sixteen Artists/Photographers*, Akron, Ohio: Art Institute, 1970, p. 16.

3. See William C. Seitz, *Art in the Age of Aquarius, 1955–1970*, compiled and edited by Marla Price, Washington, D.C.: Smithsonian Institution Press, 1992.

4. Rauschenberg included both actual photographs and reproductions in his "combine" paintings of the 1950s, and his silk-screen collages of the 1960s employed his personal photographs as well as appropriated mass-media images. In more recent years he has created his own straight, unmanipulated photographs! See "Robert Rauschenberg: 'Artist'," *Newsletter*, Photo Society, Daytona Beach (Florida) Community College, (Spring/Summer 1983): 10–11. Publications of Rauschenberg's photographs include *Photos In + Out City Limits*, Boston, ca. 1981; and *Robert Rauschenberg, Photographs*, New York: Pantheon Books, 1981.

5. Jonathan Green, *American Photography: A Critical History, 1945 to the Present*, New York: Harry N. Abrams, 1984, p. 159. Although Green has little to say about Betty Hahn specifically, one of her Lone Ranger images is reproduced as a slide on the book's dust jacket and title page.

6. David E. Halberstich [sic], "Which History of Photography Is Best?" *Popular Photography* 59, no. 1 (July 1966): 75ff. The misspelling of the author's name was acknowledged in a letter from editor H. M. Kinzer ("Mea culpa!" he wrote), but never in the magazine. At this point, review the first page of this article and the Table of Contents of this book, where I trust the name is spelled correctly.

7. H. W. Janson, *History of Art*, 3rd ed., revised and expanded by Anthony F. Janson, New York: Harry N. Abrams; and Englewood Cliffs, N.J.: Prentice-Hall, 1986, pp. 613–17, 661–65, 768–84. I am confident that the dust-jacket hype's claim that the book includes a "comprehensive treatment of the history of photography as an art form" would have been explosively denounced by Henry Holmes Smith. The artists include Uelsmann, Minor White, and Aaron Siskind, but not Smith or Hahn. That Anthony Janson's last word in the book is about photographs (the work of painter David Hockney) represents something of a pyrrhic victory for photography. I would balance it with a discussion of Betty Hahn!

8. See James Enyeart and Nancy Solomon, eds., *Henry Holmes Smith, Collected Writings 1935–1985*, Tucson: Center for Creative Photography, University of Arizona, ca. 1986. The work of Howard Bossen provides valuable insight into the provocative inquiry which characterized Smith's teaching and writing. See his article, "Dialogue of Differences: The Writing of Henry Holmes Smith," *Camera Lucida* 5 (1982): 2–23, with its many references to specific Smith texts; also his book, *Henry Holmes Smith: Man of Light*, Ann Arbor, Mich.: UMI Research Press, ca. 1983.

9. Henry Holmes Smith, "Solarization Process: For Unique and Sensational Effects," *Minicam Monthly* 3, no. 2 (October 1939): 26–31, 78–91, illustrated.

10. Susan Cohen, catalog essay in *Time After Time, The Photo-*

graphs of Alice Wells, Rochester, N.Y.: Visual Studies Workshop, 1990 (a Visual Studies Workshop Traveling Exhibition), p. 2 of unpaginated book.

11. Betty Hahn, interviews with author in Hahn's home, Albuquerque, May 11–13, 1993. Tape recording in Archives Center, National Museum of American History. All subsequent quotations and paraphrased statements attributed to Hahn are from this series of interviews and conversations, if not otherwise cited or identified.

12. Bunnell was skeptical of my involvement with Henry Smith in pursuit of a Ph.D. in the history of photography. In a letter to me (November 9, 1963), he reviewed unfavorably Smith's work in the history and theory of photography, concluding that the results were not commensurate with the amount of agonizing and fanfare which accompanied them. Bunnell was addressing the issue of Smith as art historian and observed that his work did not fit the traditional methodology taught at Yale University; also, Smith's reputation as a cantankerous hothead did not encourage fair analysis. Although Bunnell's criticisms of Smith's unfinished projects may have been well taken, for he was more critic than historian by orientation, Bunnell used the wrong yardstick to measure Smith's relative success or stature as writer and teacher. Smith was far from completing his contributions to photography in 1963: much more was to issue from his fertile mind as art, criticism and theory, and general influence. Any re-evaluation of American photography must acknowledge his importance.

13. Jack Welpott has used this term specifically in relation to Smith, and Howard Bossen in turn adopted it in writing about Smith. See Bossen, "Dialogue of Differences," op. cit., pp. 3, 21 (note 7).

14. I wish I had offered photographic instruction to my colleagues and professors myself, slyly suggesting that it was not necessary to bother someone of Henry's caliber with such a mundane chore. At this same meeting, incidentally, Professor Roy Sieber (currently associate director of the Smithsonian Institution's National Museum of African Art) dismissed student complaints about tough oral examinations with a stern remark: "Look—I'll spoon-feed you, but I won't breast-feed you!" (He no longer recalls this but agreed to take my

word for it. This is merely a marginal anecdote, but as a proponent of footnote humor, I add it in the same spirit of humor that Betty Hahn or Robert Fichter add to their work. Besides, as Dave Barry would say, I swear I am not making this up.)

15. A one-page statement entitled "Reading the Photograph" appeared in Smith's self-published pamphlet, *On Photography*, 1953 (p. 7), and the theory introduced here was developed in later writings. The problem of reading or interpreting photographs in nonliteral ways occupied him for the rest of his life.

16. Betty Hahn, untitled, undated paper on Henry Holmes Smith in her files.

17. "Sometimes, On Tuesdays, I Dream of Henry," reproduced in *Untitled* 2 and 3 (Friends of Photography, 1972–73): 78; sequence of Smith with Newhall at Creative Experience Workshop, Carmel, California, August 1972, photographed by Arne Folkedal, reproduced in same issue, p. 53.

18. Betty Hahn, "Henry Holmes Smith: Speaking with a Genuine Voice," *Image* 16, no. 4 (December 1973): 1–6, reviewing his fifty-year retrospective of September 1973.

19. See Cohen, *Time After Time*, eleventh page. I became personally aware of the complexities when I visited Robert and Betty in Rochester in 1966, as Alice and Daniel's overnight guest, sharing meals and conversation with Alice, Daniel, Betty, Robert, other visitors, and Alice's teen-aged son. Since Alice used the surname Andrews, I assumed, as did others, that they were legally husband and wife. I was surprised, disconcerted, and amused to see that Alice seemed to be carrying on a blatant affair with Robert, holding hands under the table during a spaghetti dinner. During the lively conversation, Dan, who had delightful comic gifts and a quick wit, wagged a finger at Alice to make a point. With mock solemnity, he slowly began to say, "Mrs.—" I assumed he would say "Mrs. Andrews," but out tumbled "Mrs. Fichter." We laughed nervously at the Freudian slip, but my face would have been less red had I known that Daniel and Alice were unmarried. At this time I also observed that Betty and Dan had a close friendship.

20. Ibid.

21. Ibid., note 51. A more recent exposition of Lyons's ideas is found in Robert Hirsch, "Nathan Lyons on the Snapshot" (interview transcription based on discussions September 9 and 23, 1992), *CEPA* [Center for Exploratory and Perceptual Art, Buffalo, N.Y.] (Winter 1992–93): 4 pp., unpaginated.

22. Technically, this may be true, although there was a part-time woman lecturer in the School of Photography when I was a student there, before Shoemaker's chairmanship.

23. Interview with Donald R. Lehmbeck, senior physicist, Xerox Corporation, July 24, 1993, Rochester, N.Y. Lehmbeck is a Rochester Institute of Technology photographic science graduate (1963), who taught part-time at R.I.T. briefly and knew the photographic science faculty well. My speculations were confirmed by Sandra Meek-Greenberg, picture editor, *America Illustrated* (interview, Washington, D.C., September 9, 1993). Ms. Greenberg was the only woman in her R.I.T. photography class and worked part-time for several faculty members, who could easily have hired her male classmates instead, she pointed out; she was also an *Aperture* magazine assistant to Minor White while he was an R.I.T. lecturer. She recalls Shoemaker as a kindly, jovial extrovert who hated to hurt anyone's feelings.

24. Ann Zimmerman, "An Interview with Betty Hahn," undated, in Hahn's files.

25. Statement, *Center Quarterly* [Catskill Center for Photography] 4, no. 4 (1983): 4, related to an exhibition series on "Women and Their [Role] Models." This concept is of minimal relevance, as it really constituted putting words in the photographer's mouth; she seemed to be discussing influences, not actual role models.

26. The exhibitions, which I directed, formed a series entitled "Women, Cameras, and Images": they included "I. Imogen Cunningham" (1968); "II. Betty Hahn and Gayle Smalley" (1969); "III. Berenice Abbott" (1969); and "IV. Barbara Morgan" (1969), documented in poster-catalogs by myself. Additional exhibitions were envisioned, which would have been group shows on specific themes or styles, with each photographer represented by ten to twelve images. A one-woman show in 1970, "Janine Nièpce," was not part of the series.

27. I often wish I had given her a solo show, but perhaps I feared taking a risk with a new photographer in our conservative museum (or possible criticism for giving a one-woman show to a graduate school classmate), so I combined her with Gayle Smalley as a buffer. Gayle was an R.I.T. graduate and another Henry Holmes Smith student, whom I did not know. Except for a few forceful, amusing pieces, including a satirical attack on Ronald Reagan, Smalley's work was somewhat weaker, less accomplished than Betty's.

28. A. D. Coleman, "Shows We've Seen," *Popular Photography* 73, no. 2 (August 1973): 75. Coleman found Hahn's stitched pieces more appealing than Bea Nettles's and Keith Smith's work in the same genre, and that Hahn's work retains its "charm" on repeated viewings.

29. David Haberstich, *The Camera and the Human Facade*, exhibition checklist, Washington, D.C.: Division of Photographic History, 1970.

30. The phrase alludes to an important exhibition directed by Tom Muir Wilson which opened at the Akron Art Institute in April 1970, "Into the 70's." Betty Hahn was cited as one of the leading contemporary photographic artists whose reputations had been firmly established in the 1960s. See the catalog, *Into the 70's: Photographic Images by Sixteen Artists/Photographers*, Akron, Ohio: Art Institute, 1970.

31. Robert A. Sobieszek, "Gum-Bichromate Sentiments and Stitched Stuff," introduction to exhibition checklist, undated.

32. Colleen Kenyon, "Betty Hahn—A Research Paper," unpublished paper from Rochester Institute of Technology art history seminar, May 7, 1973.

33. Van Deren Coke, "60s Continuum, *Image* 15, no. 1 (March 1972): 1–6. William Jenkins, "Some Thoughts on 60s Continuum," in the same issue, pp. 15–18.

34. V. B. Price, "Looking Alive in Albuquerque," newspaper review in Hahn's files, date not recorded.

35. Steve Yates, essay, *Betty Hahn: Inside and Outside* (August 31 to October 7, 1988, exhibition catalog), Bethlehem, Penn.: Lehigh University Art Galleries, 1988, pp. 4–8.

36. Vera Norwood, "'Thank You for My Bones': Connections Between Contemporary Women Artists and the Traditional Arts of Their Foremothers," December 1979, pp. 3–4. Jerald Maddox made the analogy of naive photography with folk art, noting its stylistic influence on "creative" photographers: "Photography as Folk Art," *One Hundred Years of Photographic History: Essays in Honor of Beaumont Newhall,* ed. by Van Deren Coke, Albuquerque: University of New Mexico Press, 1975, pp. 103–8.

37. Quoted in Henry Horenstein, "Gumming Up Their Works," American Photographer 15, no. 21 (August 1985): 66–75. See also: *The Alternative Image: An Aesthetic and Technical Exploration of Nonconventional Photographic Printing Processes,* John Michael Kohler Arts Center, Sheboygan, Wis.; and Paul Sutinen, "Made-over mug shots of mums," Visual Arts, Portland, Oregon, December 26, 1978. Horenstein's article is a good survey of several gum printers, even if Hahn is described as simply "an early" gum enthusiast. (My earliest awareness of a revival of the gum-bichromate process was in 1965, when Joel Snyder demonstrated it at George Eastman House, the same year in which Betty began to employ it.) Incidentally, the image of Robert Fichter appears in a work by Darryl Curran, reproduced in Horenstein's article. The photogenic Fichter face can be detected in many works by Hahn, Alice Wells [Andrews], and others, pictorial evidence of the close interaction and almost incestuous cross-fertilization among these artists during this period.

38. Les Krims, *The Incredible Case of the Stack o'Wheats Murders,* a Limited Edition Folio, no imprint, 1972: one of several small portfolios of reproductions which he distributed in the early 1970s.

39. Janie Cohen, catalog essay, *Betrayal of Means/Means of Betrayal,* Daytona Beach, Florida: Southeast Museum of Photography, Daytona Beach Community College, 1993, passim, but especially pp. 5 and 16–17. Cohen notes that the artists in this exhibition, including the Starn twins, try to discover "what photography does." This is a nice expansion of Smith's quest to determine "what a photograph should look like" and Lyons's interest in defining "photographic."

RIDING THE RANGE

The Straight Photographs of Betty Hahn

DANA ASBURY

There are so many dimensions to the possibilities . . . so many options . . . so many ways of arranging the pieces."
JOHN LE CARRÉ, *Tinker, Tailor, Soldier, Spy*[1]

THE WEST IS NOT BIG ENOUGH FOR THE RANGE of Betty Hahn's photographic work. To characterize her work is to come up with a list of contradictions. Her photographs are as manipulated as stitched images on fabric using nonsilver processes, as straight as the single-exposure 20x24 Polaroid; as casual as a snapshot made with a toy camera, as careful and arranged as a botanical layout; as straightforward as the documenting of a six-page letter, as enigmatic as a dream sequence on a Tokyo street. Betty Hahn uses found imagery as much as she uses her own meticulously laid-out constructions. She uses glamorous color as much as a dead-pan version of black and white. In the body of work presented here, which covers over twenty-five years, though, one does of course find threads that tie her many series together—a wry sense of humor, a designer's interest in arrangement, an ironic commentary on photographs in their relation to popular culture, and the relation of popular culture to art. She brings all manner of influences to her imagery, quoting from both "high art"—Dutch seventeenth-century still life painting, *trompe l'oeil* painting, flower paintings from the Edo period in Japan and well as ones by Piet Mondrian—and from "low art"—family albums, stitched samplers, television imagery. Only an exhibit of this size could do justice to a body of work this diverse.

In the course of her visual training, Betty Hahn came late to photography. She started studying painting, drawing, graphic design, and film-making at Indiana University and took a photography course only as a requirement. At first, she found making photographs of little interest but took it

(opposite) *16. Detail*, Albuquerque, NM (white horse head), *from the series* Passing Shots, *1978, Ektacolor photograph, 15 1/4 x 15 1/4.*

up somewhat in earnest when she moved to New York City in the summer of 1963. She discovered the camera as a "portable" medium and one well suited to capturing the wealth of stimulus she found in New York.

A critical factor in Betty Hahn's photographic studies is her work with Henry Holmes Smith, the legendary and influential teacher whose primary goal was to confound all assumptions about what a photograph should look like. His philosophy of teaching was, in Hahn's words, "expansive and open-minded." He "had enormous confidence in the medium, that it could handle anything," which he passed on to her.[2] Despite David Haberstich's detailed account of Smith's influence on Betty Hahn, it is worth quoting Smith here because his approach to the teaching of photography tells a great deal about Hahn's belief in the versatility of photography.

My commitment to teaching photography involves first, an attempt to develop respectful, constructive and imaginative attitudes towards the scope of the medium; second, to build an appreciation of the important photographic work that we know about today; and third, encourage in the student photographer a sense of freedom and dependence on himself that will permit him to face whatever challenges and opportunities may confront him as the result of either his future development or lack of it; fourth, to encourage any possibilities for technical virtuosity that may be in evidence while the student is with me.[3]

Hahn describes Henry Holmes Smith as "relentlessly brilliant, articulate, always had something to say about everything, sensitive, caring, patient, and intense, a passion for photography, intellectually adventurous, thinking off-beat, and frequently radical."[4] In his campaigning for a broader range of acceptable forms of photography, he worked with some remarkable artists who have done much to change the rules in late twentieth-century photography, including, along with Betty Hahn, Robert Fichter, Jerry Uelsmann, and Jack Welpott. Smith had a profound effect on Betty Hahn, giving her, above all, permission to make her own way and to break with convention wherever possible. All her many varied series do question in some way the nature of photography itself, whether through the choice of imagery or the back and forth tension between the imagery and the form it has taken.

Hahn began her photographic career as one of the principal instigators in the revival of nineteenth-century nonsilver techniques, including gum bichromate, Van Dyke, and cyanotype printing. In many of her early works, she relied on images from family albums and snapshots, and the interest in snapshots carried over into one of her longest-running series, *Passing Shots*.

From 1975 to 1986, Betty Hahn added images to this series, all 15 1/4-inch square color prints, made with the toy Mick-a-Matic camera. As the title implies, they are snapshots often made on the artist's travels throughout the U.S. —in California, Arizona, Florida, Hawaii—abroad in Spain, Portugal, Australia, and Japan, and close to home, with pictures from Albuquerque, Truth or Consequences, the Bosque del Apache. They are outdoor views typical of tourist pictures, some distant views of landscapes but many just pure enjoyment of color, shape, and atmosphere (Fig. 17). There is a fluorescent gold fish in a pool of dark green water, exotic banana plants in Lisbon, a lush garden of flowers in Kyoto. This cannot be "serious" work—it was made by a tourist and, what's more, with a toy camera. It has the soft focus of a plastic lens and amateur framing evident in, for example, the cut-off head of a bright flamingo. These pictures were made "in passing," as notes, sensual mementos of birds, flowers, and lily ponds encountered on many journeys.

The snapshot aesthetic is the basis of a good portion of all the photographs ever made, though to call it an "aesthetic" is to endow snapshot photographers with more self-consciousness than is warranted. The true amateur snapshot was made to be a record; the creation of a memory was more important than what the photograph looked like, as long as the person or event being documented was really there in the frame. The true snapshot is made by someone without visual training. For an artist like Betty Hahn to make snapshots with a toy camera is both a rejection and an expansion of the accepted notion of what a photograph should look like. The use of toy cameras became popular among art photographers in the late 1970s—but Betty Hahn was using the Mick-a-Matic earlier than that, as a free-minded way of bringing the practice of sketching to photography. The sense of quickness and ease in these

17. Palm Shadow, Garden of the Alcazar, Seville, *from the series* Passing Shots, *1983, Ektacolor photograph, 15 1/4 x 15 1/4.*

photographs belies a sophistication and self-consciousness that true snapshots lack, by definition. When printed fifteen inches square, matted, framed, and hung on the wall, the images from *Passing Shots* take on a bold aesthetic presence and beauty that no toy camera manufacturer ever dreamed of.

During the 1960s artists and curators both began to reexamine different genres of photographs in an effort to get away from restrictive definitions of what makes a photo-

18. Botanical Layout: Carnation, 1988, Polacolor II photograph, 24 x 20.

graph "art." Nathan Lyons notes that in the late 1950s when he first went to the George Eastman House in Rochester, the collection there was divided into three parts: the A collection was fine photographs by fine photographers, the

B collection not-so-fine photographs by lesser-known photographers, and the C collection anonymous images, including snapshots and vernacular images. Needless to say, he found the most puzzling and challenging images in the C collection.[5] Lyons raises the question of whether a trained artist can even make a snapshot but says,

> A challenging imagemaker can make most anything work. It may work for different reasons than the original snapshot did in the original sense. The genesis of the whole notion of snapshooting had to do with the idea of hunting. The terminology extends from the idea of a spontaneous reaction to circumstance without any pre-thoughts or preconsideration. A number of people embraced some of the characteristics, issues, and attitudes and incorporated them into their work. It was not an emulation of style, but something that fit their needs of expression.[6]

Embracing the "flaws" of snapshots was a way of bypassing the high-art demands of serious photography. The pictures in *Passing Shots* are liberated from the subject matter and the technical look of the fine print, but their apparent casualness is deceptive. Bold, graphic compositions and a sophisticated use of light and shadow confound the expectations of the snapshot itself and make this a multilayered play back and forth between genres and assumptions. Is Betty Hahn making mementos from her travels, or art photographs? She is doing both, or doing neither; she is having fun, in passing.

To view the *Passing Shots* series along with the roughly contemporaneous *Botanical Layouts* is to find the essential polarities present throughout Betty Hahn's career. The *Botanical Layouts* are as meticulous as the snapshots are casual. They are laborious rather than speedy, carefully constructed rather than found and informal. They are made with the state-of-the-art 20x24 Polaroid camera, of which there are only a few in existence, as opposed to the mass-produced Mick-a-matic available for less than ten dollars.

Leaves and flowers are the recurring motif in this series, as they were in *Passing Shots*. Of course, they are no longer plein-air views, a traveler's delectation of the world, but indoor studio shots, specimens laid out for examination, sometimes on a decorative background, like flowered wallpaper, but more often on a neutral gray background. Added are carefully drawn diagrams of leaves and other parts. They are deliberately reminiscent of botanical prints of the nineteenth century, when science was a glorious exercise in the accumulation of detail, and in botany the whole theory of classification was reborn with the publication in 1859 of Darwin's *Origin of Species* (Fig. 18).

Betty Hahn is a master at choosing subjects loaded with content and connotation and then, in her cool approach, draining them of that content. Flowers are universal symbols; they carry connotations of fragility, delicacy, femininity. They are embodiments of romanticism's exaltation of organic form. Hahn's flower pictures—whether from *Passing Shots* or *Botanical Layouts*—are "fearlessly decorative." It was Henry Holmes Smith who gave her this courage to rely

on her senses. In the *Botanical Layouts,* Betty Hahn provides what appears to be information—the diagrams and identifying numbers, for example—but there is no key. They are like footnote numbers without the sources. Photography is a medium characterized by the presentation of pseudo-information—an accumulation of facts that may or may not be revealing—and nowhere is this more dramatic than in representation by the 20x24 Polaroid camera. We have detail presented larger than life, in sharper focus than the eye can see, in vibrant color that already resides in the paper and is released by that final act of exposure. But what more can we learn from these crystalline images? Does all this hyperrealism reveal anything? What information is here in this detail that is not in the dreamy *Passing Shots*?

Betty Hahn plays with this question while making stunning prints. The *Botanical Layouts* are large and decorative, and, at first glance, easy on the eye. *House and Garden* magazine found them alluring enough to include an article about them on a page labeled "Events of exceptional interest in the arts, design, entertainment, and living."[7] Flowers are a classic subject, like the landscape or the nude. However, upon closer examination, these photographs are not quite what they seem. Hahn says, "Whatever it is, I can't put my finger on it, but the *Botanical Layouts* have something a little too anatomical about them. They're like an autopsy—they have that edge that makes them more than just elegant pictures of flowers."[8] The theme of autopsy performed by the camera comes up later in Betty Hahn's crime photography. Here, though, in these beautiful layouts, we can marvel

19. Chicago Family: Grandmother, 1979, *Polacolor II photograph,* 24 x 20.

at the jewel-like qualities of photographic representation and, not yet anyway, have much reason to look on them with suspicion.

The hyperrealism of the large-format Polaroid does lend a totemic quality to these examinations, as if they were ritual objects with magical powers. The Polaroid camera gave

Hahn her first experience with what she calls "precision" photography, as opposed to the out-of-focus negatives and the results of a toy camera with which she was more familiar. It was an astonishing change for her, and in considering the question of what to do with this format, she decided to make use of photography's remarkable ability to inventory. In two compositions entitled *Chicago Family: Grandmother,* 1979 (Fig. 19), and *Aunt,* 1980, Hahn has gathered snapshots, newspaper clippings, mementos, and artifacts and arranged them carefully against a black watered silk background, to present a life, or a tribute. These are still lifes in the French sense—*nature morte,* stilled life. They are like altarpieces, full of references to time past and symbols of life's brevity—flowers again, butterflies, dead birds—and numerous references to life in Chicago in the 1940s. They have an obsessive quality to them, as if the laying out of artifacts—and tucking them into a ribbon grid—can sum up a life, or depict something of its meaning. Mostly, though, they are a reminder that all the camera can really do is record these details endlessly; *Chicago Family* is a photograph of photographs; the reproduction in this book a photograph of a photograph of photographs; it can go on forever as we gather and save bits of paper, and keep looking more closely at generations of reproduction, looking for more clues.

These compositions are also reminiscent of nineteenth-century American *trompe l'oeil* still life paintings, especially the rack paintings of John Frederick Peto (1854–1907). The rack painting represents an old but not very common still life tradition that dates back to the sixteenth century. It was resurrected with one or two well-known paintings by William Harnett, from whom Peto took his cue and painted dozens more. He was, notes art historian Alfred Franken-stein, the master of the rack painting,[9] a subject that lended itself well to his interest in the simple, humble, and ordinary subjects common to *trompe l'oeil* still lifes. Peto's rack paintings, like *Chicago Family,* evoke a sense of narrative without actually providing the details (Fig. 20). The illusion-ary assemblages of letters, calling cards, and other printed ephemera look as though they should be legible, but they are not. We have the forbidden pleasure—almost—of being able to read someone else's mail, or, in Peto's highly person-al signboard paintings, of bearing witness to his affections for family and friends. Hahn's works, like Peto's, are im-bued with the Victorian enjoyment of bric-a-brac as well as a Victorian's delight in the new availability of printed mass media—in the forms of picture postcards and calling cards, as well as serialized stories, paperback novels, and so on. People had a passion for all these new sources of informa-tion and entertainment in late nineteenth-century America. Peto had a talent for painting that passion in his illusionis-tic, photographic manner, but oddly, to Hahn at least, his racks were always full of the collections of men. In her ex-perience it was much more frequently women who save all those mementos and letters and dance cards, and she was interested in what the women in her own family had care-fully stored away. The poignance of those treasured scraps is emphasized by the warm golden light in which they are photographed.

20. *John Frederick Peto,* The Rack, *1880, oil on canvas, 24 x 20. Courtesy Arizona State University, Tempe; gift of Oliver B. James.*

The tradition of *trompe l'oeil* painting obviously owes much to photography, but it is also indebted to its seven-teenth-century Dutch precedents when the subject matter of still life paintings reflected an emerging fascination with the things and activities of the everyday world. If there ever was an American national style, John Wilmerding has observed that still life painting of the late nineteenth century bears evidence of one in its overall concern for the practical and the functional.[10] An interest in mundane subjects combines with the debate between high art and low as a recurrent theme in American art and in photography both, and one that plays throughout the work of Betty Hahn. Kirk Varnedoe and Adam Gopnick's important 1990 catalogue and exhibition *High and Low: Modern Art and Popular Culture* traces the embracing of popular culture as subject matter for artists since the beginning of this century and show it to be an exploration of substance and depth. In the "apparently trivial and marginal things taken for granted ... was an alphabet for art's new language," they note,[11] a whole new way of making reference to a modern subculture. Finding inspiration in popular imagery is frequently accompanied by an unstated critique of that popular culture, a finger pointed sourly at the shallowness. Sourness, however, is not part of Betty Hahn's lexicon. No artist has gathered all these references and ephemeral artifacts with more pure enjoyment and wit than she has.

One of the long-term effects of working with the Polaroid camera for Hahn was that it inspired her interest in—and made her more comfortable with—straight photography. The straightforward recording of artifacts would become a primary theme in her numerous series of the 1980s; one of the loveliest and most understated of her works is the series *A Japanese Collage in 5 Parts,* 1988 (Plate 113). Beautifully simple stacks of papers fill the frame from edge to edge, the

only other elements a strip of paper across the center with five Japanese characters, a carefully chosen, intense background color, and the delicate roller marks of excess emulsion at the top of the print. These are as spare as compositions can be; they are ready-made studies of color, form, and pattern, and all the artist needs to do in this case is to look at them with the intensity this camera's lens provides to give them their monumental floating presence. These Japanese papers are exotic and ordinary at the same time, and they hang in the balance between art and fact. In marked contrast to many of her other Polaroid still lifes in their spareness, they are stripped down to minimal elements. To call them "collages" belies their austerity. Like *Passing Shots,* these prints are pure observation, just "shape management," as Hahn says about *Passing Shots.* But because of the format, you can see the individual threads in these delicate papers; their texture is palpable. They also share with much of Hahn's other work a delight in all kinds of pieces of paper—the kind of delight and understanding of its inherent interest Peto showed in the rack paintings, and that underlies *Chicago Family.*

Many of her series rest on this interest in ephemera, including the seven-part series *Letter from the Chelsea Hotel,* in which Hahn enlarges and presents a personal letter, taped together in one part, scrawled on Chelsea Hotel stationery, along with its envelope (Plates 107–9). There is nothing grand about this series; it is about the humbleness of the subject matter—and the humble, though legendary status

6 or 7 clues connected
to a case involving
contributory negligence

Seven Clues series, also 20 x 24 Polaroid prints, are arrange-ments of facts—three-dimensional objects with provocative qualities—evidence that may or may not add up to some-thing, that may or not provide useful information (Fig. 21). Plastic bags contain the pieces—a hotel room key, a busi-ness card, a coffee mug (with fingerprints? with a "G" that means something?). It's up to the viewer—just as it is up to the detective—to make up the story or fill in the blanks. The viewer, though, must also fill in the crime, which is clearly indicated but left vague. Hahn is keenly aware that one only needs to put an ordinary object—a pair of eye-glasses, say—into a plastic bag and call it a clue to give it ominous overtones. A single shoe, which shows up in Hahn's imagery as frequently and inexplicably as it does in real life, automatically connotes mystery. It is loaded with meaning. Why is it that so often a single shoe is left in the street? What terrible thing can happen to a person to make him—or even more ominously, her—lose one shoe?

Fiction in any form has always intended to be realistic.
—RAYMOND CHANDLER

21. *6 or 7 clues connected to a case involving contributory negligence, 1980, Polacolor II photograph, 24 x 20.*

of the Chelsea Hotel as a hang-out for artists and drifters, and the romanticized allure of being creative and poor in New York City.

    The leap from Betty Hahn's still life photographs to the crime series is not such a large one, given the clinical ap-proach that characterizes the *Botanical Layouts*. The *Six or*

AROUND THIS TIME, Hahn notes mischievously that her subscription to *Artforum* ran out and she began getting *True Detective* and *Front Page Detective* instead. She joined the Evidence Photographers International Council and went to a seminar on the West Coast that discussed, among vari-ous topics, the coroner's use of photography and crime lab photography. What interested her most about the approach of evidence photographers was the thoroughness for exploring different viewpoints through the photographs. Hahn says, "I like the way evidence photography looks, but also what the pictures do. They have a real job to do. An artist would call the image a still life, but it's not. It has a past, tells a story. It's loaded with information."[12] "Information" is everywhere, everything potentially a clue. She says, "I see everything now as evidence. When the light levels go down I see almost any situation as one that could be a scene of a crime (almost always isn't, but could be)."[13]

Tapping into the roots of popular consciousness is a unifying thread throughout Betty Hahn's work, and her identification of herself, of the photographer, with the detective figure—a true twentieth-century popular hero—is canny. Throughout the crime series Hahn plays with the idea of the interchangeability of the detective, the criminal, and the artist. The detective novel as a genre is a particularly apt parallel for photography. Detective fiction—like Hahn's photographs—is a kind of game, a serious one governed by strict conventions of the genre. The inherent order of the world is assumed; its essential morality asserted and reasserted. The world in detective fiction—and in Betty Hahn's crime photographs—is a closed and orderly system. Irrationality and sensationalism are missing. The photographer takes a deliberate, systematic approach, lays out the evidence, photographs the clues one by one, and eventually the truth will be revealed. The detective, said Ellery Queen, is a prophet looking backwards. So too is the photographer.

The parallels between detective fiction and photography go further. Both occur after the event. Photographs are literally and metaphorically *after the fact,* as is detective fiction. It is the fact—the crime—that gives it a *raison d'être,* and the rest is retrospective, piecing together the story from the clues. The detective, like the artist, is essentially a romantic figure, an individualist, often an outsider looking in, one who sees more than the ordinary person. For a detective, or a photographer, to solve a crime requires creativity and imagination. The detective is a visionary, but he or she sees into the past, rather than into the future. Detectives and artists both see patterns where other people see only isolated facts, they both reveal and make intelligible what would otherwise be dark.

It's noteworthy how often the setting of violence looks as unconvincing as an amateur theatrical. . . .
—CAPTION FOR A PHOTOGRAPH IN
The Other Churchill: The Story of an Expert Witness

THE SERIES *A Case of XX* (1981) presents the scene of a crime as it would appear to an investigator, in a nonlinear assortment of views that doesn't really delineate the story of a crime but certainly depicts all the conventions of one (Plate 116). The usual array of clues is here: fingerprints, tell-tale signs in the dumpster in an alley, a trace of something suspicious that stained the floor. The caption frames underscore the conventions of the genre with the language of the hardboiled gumshoe.

She dropped her cigarette on the floor and stepped on it. 'Here comes the crazy part,' she said. 'At night the stove gives enough light so you can see.' *Having determined which are the customary objects in a room, it follows that all other objects have been placed on the scene recently and should be carefully inspected. The condition and contents of fireplaces and waste baskets may throw light on what has recently happened. Obviously these details must fit into the picture and help account for what has occurred. A systematic general survey should be used in describing the scene of the crime."* [Image #28 from *A Case of XX*]

This is the self-conscious language of crime fiction, reversed out in white on black to emphasize its starkness, its very qualities of black and white. Betty Hahn has managed to give us the surface of crime fiction without its real substance. "At night the stove gives enough light so you can see." Is this a revelatory observation? Does it have any relationship to the words that follow it? Of course no tool is more useful for a systematic general survey than the camera, and yet how remarkably little it is really able to tell us. Is the camera a faithful witness or a faithless one? We cannot rely on Betty Hahn here either—she is criminal, investigator, and artist all at once—to let us know. But, as she learned in *Homicide Investigation: Practical Information for Coroners, Police Officers, and Other Investigators,* "If a murder investigation ends in failure, the cause is usually an inadequate examination of the scene of the crime."

"It is not a fragrant world, but it is the world you live in, and certain writers with tough minds and a cool spirit of detachment can make very interesting and even amusing patterns out of it. It is not funny that a man should be killed, but it sometimes funny that he should be killed for so little, and that his death should be the coin of what we call civilization."
—RAYMOND CHANDLER, FROM *The Simple Art of Murder*

THE *Crime in the Home* SERIES offers with deadpan humor an assortment of clues that reveal a criminal at work. Hahn uses the conventions of forensic photography—the arrow pointing out the details we lay people might miss (even though frequently in her work an arrow points to nothing), the ruler for a sense of scale—to accumulate the evidence and create an airtight case against the perp, a sketch of whom is presented in the last frame of the series (Fig. 22). Even though the crime here is not murder, it is a chewed shoe, a frayed rug, the investigation is no less serious. This is the Dragnet approach: tough, serious, thorough. No crime was too small for Sergeant Friday and his partner, Officer Bill Gannon.

It is no coincidence that the great tradition of detective fiction has its roots in the mid-nineteenth century; in fact, the detective as a modern hero came about around the same time as the invention of photography. Hahn recalls that one of the first books she read as a child was *The Adventures of Sherlock Holmes.* The mid-nineteenth century was, as mentioned above, a time of great regard for and belief in science. The detective was one who put the scientific method to

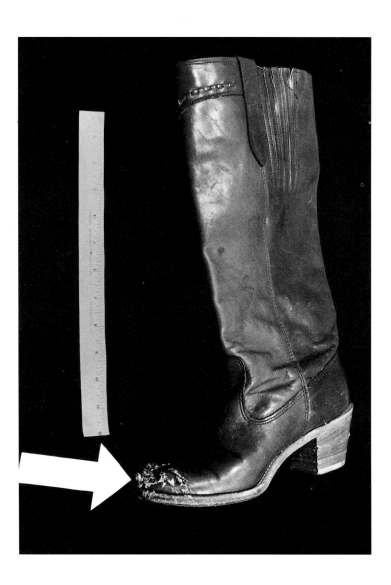

22. Exhibit G: Cowboy Boot Assaulted, *from the series* Crime in the Home, *1982, color (Cibachrome) photograph, 14 x 11.*

work, taking a calm, orderly approach to the chaos represented by crime. He represents the triumph of the mind, of rational thought, over the baser inclinations of human nature. Science itself was considered a systematic form of detection, just as photography was suspended for so long between being an art and a science. Whereas the debate over whether photography is an art may have long since been dropped, the tension between the straightforward, factual, pseudoscientific look of photographs and the notion of art as imagination is one that Betty Hahn uses with skill.

In the *Scenes of Crime* photographs, we enter a darker and more menacing world, where the crime, still mostly unnamed, goes beyond a chewed up cowboy boot (Fig. 23). There are connections between a well-planned crime and a work of art. As Thomas DeQuincey said in his essay, "On Murder Considered as One of the Fine Arts" (1827), "People begin to see that something more goes into the composition of a fine murder than two blockheads to kill or be killed, a knife, a purse, and a dark lane. Design, gentleman, grouping, light and shade, poetry, sentiment, are now deemed indispensable to attempts of this nature."[14] DeQuincey also noted that villains doing battle with the great detectives "are often in some perverse sense artists."[15] The theme of the artist as detective/the detective as artist runs throughout the series of photographs as evidence and points to Betty Hahn's self-conscious handling of the many strains of popular culture referred to in her work.

A later work, *Teddy Bear* (1988) is a two-part Polaroid showing an old photograph of a bear with his stuffing out

—stuffing which consisted of an assortment of spy cameras, miniature film cassettes, and other spy paraphernalia (Plate 112). The flip side is a typed caption taped to the back of the photograph—in German, not translated but with enough cognates for a viewer to understand the substance of it. This chilling image is as ominous as any of Hahn's crime photographs. It is a picture, probably from the Cold War-era, about a world of deception, where nothing is as it seems.

In 1982, Hahn made an eight-part series entitled *Ehrlichman Surveillance* in which she tracked John Ehrlichman at an outdoor gathering (Fig. 24). The series reminds us of the insidious uses to which photography has been put, calls up the world of the spy thriller, and of course has a strong dose of irony in the character under surveillance being Ehrlichman, for whose role in the many illegal activities of the Nixon Administration he had already spent his time in prison. Ehrlichman has the misfortune to be an inherently unsavory-looking character; even at what was undoubtedly an innocent backyard gathering, he looks suspicious. But Hahn knows that one only has to follow someone and spy on him to make him seem suspicious—that is what is so dangerous and so compelling about surveillance.

At least in this series, John Ehrlichman is Betty Hahn's antihero; she has a particular gift for choosing such figures with skill. Ehrlichman and his partner Bob Haldeman, once labeled the German shepherds, were overzealous protectors of a paranoid president, amoral figures in a corrupt administration, and as such symbols of a macho mentality run amok. There is something quite funny about Hahn the art-

(top) 23. Scene of the Crime, *1979, Ektacolor photograph, 8 x 10.*

(bottom) 24. Ehrlichman Surveillance, *1982, gelatin silver photograph, 16 x 24.*

ist/ investigator following Ehrlichman around, years later, spying on him with her camera. But the contrast between his crimes and her invasion of his privacy is notable; the humor is ironic in its innocence, at Ehrlichman's expense.

Focusing on an antiheroic figure is the flip side of Betty Hahn's extended study of the Lone Ranger, who was a true American hero in two dimensions and nothing but a media creation. "I am a great American," the Lone Ranger said of himself. And that, of course, was his appeal. He was created as the star of a radio show, a Robin Hood kind of character without any scruffiness and with the authoritativeness of law and order on his side. He spoke with perfect diction and had good manners. Designed to fulfill a need for fantasy and heroism for children and adults alike in the midst of the Great Depression, he was part of the dime novel and comic book tradition, and he made a successful transition to television in the late 1950s. Hahn's highly manipulated series in the seventies and eighties, *Who Was That Masked Man? I Wanted to Thank Him,"* used the Lone Ranger as an icon that reappeared in all kinds of nonsilver prints with and without hand-applied color. For some years this was Hahn's most well-known work and remains the series with the most technical variation. What began as an exercise in variation and an exploration of the possibilities available in different techniques became a long-running comment on media heroism.

Her choice of this western hero is significant in that she picked a fictional creation, rather than someone like Billy the Kid or General George Armstrong Custer, historical

characters loaded with mythical and political connotations. The Lone Ranger was a much beloved character; he fit the classic image of the western hero: a traveling loner who appears and does battle when needed, and moves on after having deeply affected those left behind. Who was that masked man? It is the quintessential question that applies to an ancient tale of a hero, a quest, a battle, and ultimately victory over evil. Every radio adventure began with this stirring proclamation:

With his faithful Indian companion Tonto, the daring and resourceful Masked Rider of the Plains led the fight for law and order in the early western United States. Nowhere in the pages of history can one find a greater champion of justice. Return with us now to those thrilling days of yesteryear. From out of the past come the thundering hoofbeats of the great horse Silver. The Lone Ranger rides again![16]

This champion of justice provided Hahn with a rich and identifiable symbol of the media hero, one drawn so broadly and with such shallowness there was little ambiguity in his message and almost none of the complexities that dogged other western heroes, especially more contemporary ones, whose relationship with civilization was a troubled one. He was so recognizable, Hahn was able to manipulate his image freely without ever compromising his identity. The Lone Ranger wasn't an outlaw, just a loner, and after all, he did have his sidekick Tonto. His values, methods, and allegiances were not in opposition to society's, he wasn't anti-Establishment, and he seemed to be always moving on simply to avoid the embarrassment of being thanked and glorified. This hero was remarkably free of cynicism, and his lack of dimension is what made his transformation into a flat, photographic symbol so successful. The strong basic visual aspects connected with the Lone Ranger—the black mask, white horse, and silver bullets—also gave this series a sturdy formal underpinning that allowed for the free experimentation.

In 1984, Hahn concluded the series with *Appearance*, a sequence of eleven photographs of Clayton Moore, the actor who played the Lone Ranger on television, coupled with narrative captions in the melodramatic style of the radio prologue (Plate 42). Moore is making his appearance in the gym at Queen of Angels Catholic grade school in Albuquerque before a rather small audience—hardly a glamorous event for a celebrity once so famous. In opposition to this mundane event is the overexcited story told in the captions, of the Lone Ranger's leave-taking. "There's still a lot of work to be done in this great West of ours, Betty, and trails seldom cross again once they're behind us." The Lone Ranger rides off into a canyon, unknowingly right into a band of stampeding wild horses. "Betty's heart leaped to her throat for fear that that masked man might be caught in that charge of the wild horse herd." The photographs show Moore talking to a polite but barely interested audience. "There, on a low shelf of rock above the canyon floor a level ray of the disappearing sun illuminated for an instant the tableau of the great white stallion and his gallant rider."

In this series, as in others, Hahn plays with the relationship between photograph and caption, here telling a dramatic story against decidedly uneventful imagery. As she describes it, there is "the reality on one track and the fantasy on the other." The Lone Ranger was a great popular hero—one whose popularity lasted many decades—but Clayton Moore is just an actor whose show most of the kids in this gym had never seen. The Lone Ranger as a polite and rather loopy hero doesn't have much to offer late-twentieth-century kids more familiar now with Rambo and the Terminator. The masked man in a white hat on a white horse seems as out of place and lost in this series of photographs as he does in the Queen of Angels gymnasium.

The additional irony is that Clayton Moore never did anything else or had any other identity. In 1979 in a dispute with Lone Ranger TV over who owned the property rights to the character, a Los Angeles Superior Court judge issued an injunction forbidding Moore from wearing the Lone Ranger mask. Of course for Moore the issue was not property rights but the essence of his existence. Although he was defeated in court, he vowed to live on. "I've portrayed the Lone Ranger for over thirty years," he said. "I shall continue to make personal appearances all over the country for my thousands of fans."[17]

John Ehrlichman was a media celebrity too, in his own way. Once he was front-page news. Hahn presents him as she does Clayton Moore: the dramatic subplot of surveillance doesn't match the banal imagery of the backyard gathering. Moore and Ehrlichman are the straight men for Hahn's offstage comedic presence. She is the spy following the has-been criminal, she the heroine saying goodbye to the Lone Ranger. She lets us know that the media frenzies on which she is commenting—but not quite recording—are mostly smoke and mirrors—and photographs.

Betty Hahn's interest in both crime photography and mysteries and in the relationship of captions to photographs led her naturally to more of an interest in narrative. The 20 x24 Polaroid camera may have given her faith in the power of the straight photograph, but it also made her realize the limitations of the single image. The series *Appearance* marked a departure in her use of sequential imagery where no particular image is required to carry the burden of plot or meaning. Hahn's investigation of photographs as fragments from a whole, more as stills from a film, draws on still other sources. Instead of crime fiction and forensic photography, the first filmic sequences have the moody raking light of film noir in the forties, and she titles *Arrival or Departure (After Hitchcock)* (Plate 117). This series of five photographs (1987) shows the back of a man, unidentified, at a deserted train station, in late afternoon light. The rest is ambiguous. Is he coming or going? Is he moving away from the viewer, or is the photographer/viewer moving away from him? Is there significance to the first close-up shot of a black duffel bag stuffed under his arm? It was, of course, Hitchcock's particular genius to explore the ominousness of everyday situations, and to show us that looking too long at *anything* makes it look suspicious. This series pays homage

to Hitchcock's use of the tracking shot that conveys his terrifying message, the same message behind *Teddy Bear,* that there is serious threat in ordinary objects. This series also fits in with the mood of *Appearance, Ehrlichman Surveillance,* and many of the crime series—the solitary male figure in an urban setting. There is a tough edge to these works. Writing at the turn of the century, G. K. Chesterton called the detective story the folktale of the modern metropolis and said in "A Defense of Detective Stories" that they are the "earliest and only form of popular literature in which is expressed some sense of the poetry of modern life."[18] Hitchcock relayed the same sense of poetry in a refusal to view anything common or prosaic as commonplace. The detective novel found its perfect pictorial complement in film noir. The dark angles, long shadows, black and white palette all contributed to the gritty and distinctive look of the era, a kind of macho gutter glamour that Betty Hahn is quoting from here.

Man Coming into Focus (1988) is another narrative sequence that uses both film conventions and aspects of camera technology (Fig. 25). The background starts out in black and white, goes to blood red in the middle of the sequence, and fades out to a sepia tone in the final image. The photograph of the man comes slowly into focus, as if by looking at it long enough it's meaning will become clear. This is a feeling that underlies much of Betty Hahn's work: *as if* the information is all there; it is simply up to us to decipher it. These film sequences are like the still lifes in a literal sense, as in *stilled life.* Though they make reference to film, it is essential that they are still photographs, frozen frames, or, as Hahn says, "trapped pieces of time." The implication of being trapped, locked into the frame-by-single-frame sequence of photographic narrative is crucial to these images. They go right up to the edge of film but are eternally left on the precipice between immutability and motion, between silence and sound track.

Hahn's more recent sequences retain their many references to film but have less of a narrative line and even more of a sense of enigma. She has abandoned the familiar and mundane settings close to home for more exotic sites around the world: a street in Tokyo, a hotel in Berlin, and these sites make the photographs reminiscent of foreign film. After exploring the essence of popular American culture—in family snapshots, in references to the essential American hero as loner, cowboy, detective, spy—she has expanded in recent years to a more international forum. Hahn says that she has always loved foreign films with subtitles; it's part of her interest in the relationship between image and caption and the fact that even though the information is *purportedly* there, something is always missing or it isn't quite right. Her series *Shinjuku* (1984), named after a bustling commercial and entertainment center in Tokyo, is Hahn's homage to Japanese film—and Japanese culture, in a larger sense, its inscrutability to Western eyes (Plate 114). This series seems to have something happening in it, but then again, perhaps not. There is a hint of story: "Last night I dreamed I was in Tokyo again. I thought I saw forbidden colors in the neon of Shinjuku. . . . Did someone try to warn me? In what lan-

25. *Frame 5 from* Man Coming into Focus, *1988, Polacolor II photograph, 24 x 20.*

guage? I can't remember." The photographs go from black and white to color, and back to black and white. There seem to be clues, but we might be missing them. A figure appears mid-series, looks directly at the camera, and then is gone. Is this a warning, or just a passerby? There are many clues here, not immediately apparent, but just beneath the surface. "Last night I dreamt I went to Manderley again" is the beginning line in *Rebecca,* by Daphne du Maurier, another of Hahn's memorable early reading experiences. Forbidden colors is a reference to a book by Yukio Mishima, who deplored the Westernization of Japanese culture and committed ritual suicide to show, among other things, the loss of ancient Samurai values. The part of Tokyo represented by Shinjuku is what Mishima abhorred most of all. This is a complex work in which Hahn is exploring the intricacies of presenting information—how to include enough, without giving too much. This work is about finding the right number of clues.

The series not only makes specific reference to a dream but is very dreamlike in its presentation of imagery. Hahn captures that feeling of timelessness, when you cannot be sure if this dream lasted all night or for a few seconds. "I sense some kind of relationship between film and dreams," Hahn says. "It is the combination of shots, the succession and relationships of images to each other, that set the stage and create the atmosphere for something more interesting."[19] It is clear that Betty Hahn does not think in terms of single photographs anymore. She does, in fact, view herself more as a designer or a director than a photographer. She does installations now rather than individual photographs.

"The overriding idea that ties my work together," Hahn observes, "is that I never do photographs that are complete statements in themselves. I'll take an essentially incomplete image, then complete it with a process—paint, drawing, fa-bric, and now text. . . . I look for incomplete or extremely simple photographs which provide an entry to play with the image as an idea or process."[20] As varied as Betty Hahn's different bodies of work are, they do all reveal a similarity of approach, this skilled way of presenting visual material to establish a tone and an atmosphere, and to call up a whole mode, whether it is foreign films or American television. One of the ultimate questions underlying all these modes, both detective fiction and family memories alike, is what is the connection between daydream and reality? It is a potent question for anyone engaged in straight photography and again brings up the notion of information purported to be there.

Two of the series made in Berlin bring together many of the threads that run throughout Betty Hahn's career, combining dreamlike sequences, a sense of narrative, and anonymous public imagery with the personal. *Circumstances of Awakening* (1990) seems to take us inside the head of a sleeping man as he approaches a state of wakefulness (Plate 115). Although he is waking up in what is probably a hotel room in this German capital, the scene shifts from the blurry early morning fog and from the black-and-white city to green tropical sites reminiscent of *Passing Shots.* The final image is a horizonless field of red flowers. We are back to Hahn's flowers and to a softer view of the world. But at the same time fields of red flowers, especially in Europe, are associated with cemeteries and with memorials to the war dead. This world is in color, though; it is no longer the tough and ironic place of lone men. Unlike most of the series, this one has a real ending, a culminating image that signals hopefulness and a sense of closure, instead of the usual dangling enigma. About her Berlin photographs Hahn has said, "I create little glimpses that tell stories of what's happening. I've always liked to look at photographs that puzzle me, where details are missing in the shadows. I do this with my work because I like viewers to contribute, to look at the pictures and try to figure things out."[21]

NOTES

1. From Betty Hahn's personal files, a quote from an inteview with John le Carré on the BBC videotape of *Tinker, Tailor, Soldier, Spy*, c. 1979.

2. John Bloom, "An Interview with Betty Hahn (1986)," in *Photography at Bay: Interviews, Essays, and Reviews* (Albuquerque: University of New Mexico Press, 1993), p. 322.

3. Pamela S. Bosch, "Henry Holmes Smith: The Influence of Ideology," unpublished paper from Betty Hahn's collection, p. 9. Smith quoted from "My Commitment to Teaching Photography," *Aperture* 11, Special Supplement (1963): 8.

4. Bosch, pp. 10–11.

5. Nathan Lyons, interview by Robert Hirsch in Center for Exploratory and Perceptual Art (CEPA) newsletter (Buffalo, N.Y.), Winter 1992–93, p. 6.

6. Ibid., p. 7.

7. *House and Garden* 155, no. 9 (September 1983).

8. Ibid.

9. *The Reminiscent Object: Paintings by William Michael Harnett, John Frederick Peto, and John Haberle*, introduction by Alfred Frankenstein [exhibition catalogue, La Jolla Museum of Art, 1965], npn [p. 3].

10. John Wilmerding, *Important Information Inside: The Art of John Frederick Peto and the Idea of Still Life Painting in Nineteenth-Century America* (New York: Harper and Row, and Washington, D.C.: National Gallery of Art, 1983), p. 37.

11. Kirk Varnedoe and Adam Gopnik, *High and Low: Modern Art and Popular Culture* (New York: Museum of Modern Art, 1990), p. 15.

12. Review in *Santa Fe New Mexican*, June 28, 1991, pp. 13, 14.

13. Quoted from "Putting the Pieces Together," on *Colores* (Albuquerque: KNME-TV), March 1992.

14. David Lehman, *The Perfect Murder: A Story in Detection* (New York: The Free Press, 1989), p. 45.

15. Ibid., p. 49.

16. Rita Parks, *The Western Hero in Film and Television* (Ann Arbor: UMI Research Press, 1982), p. 127.

17. From notes in Betty Hahn's files.

18. David Lehman, *The Perfect Murder*, p. 122.

19. Roseanne Gain, "Photo Pioneers Bourke-White and Hahn," *Santa Fe Reporter* 17, no. 1 (June 26–July 2, 1991).

20. John Bloom, *Photography at Bay*, p. 325.

21. *Santa Fe New Mexican*, June 28, 1991, pp. 13–14.

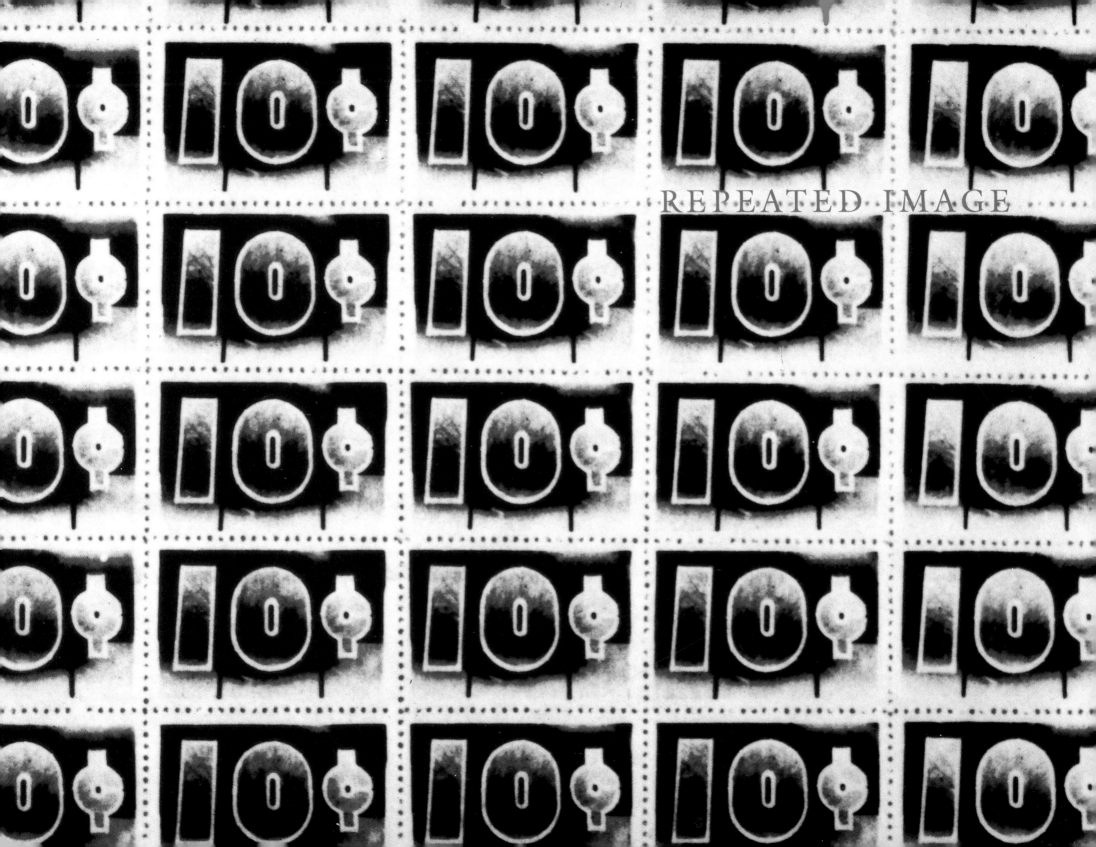

1. My Sisters-Negative and Positive, *1965, gum bichromate on paper, 15 x 22.*

2. Bather, A Senseless Duplication, *1967, gum bichromate on paper, 15 x 22.*

3. *(opposite left)* Inner Rainbow, *1968, gum bichromate on paper, 22 1/2 x 14 1/2.*

4. *(opposite right)* Processed by Kodak, *1968, gum bichromate on paper, 22 x 14.*

5. Girl by Four Highways, *1968, gum bichromate on paper, 14 x 22.*

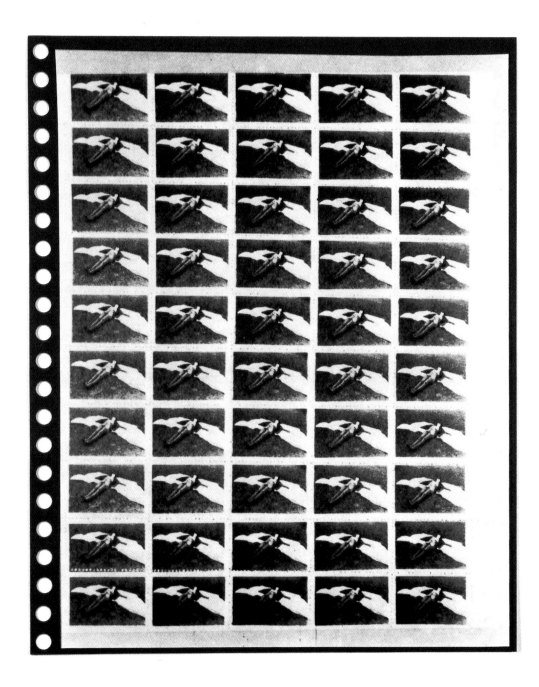

6. Airmail Stamp *(left) and* Ten Cent Stamp *(right), from the series*
Commemoratives, *1971, 3-M Color-in-Color photocopies, each 10 x 8.*

7. *(opposite)* Yard, *from the series* Commemoratives,
1971, gelatin silver photograph, 8 x 10.

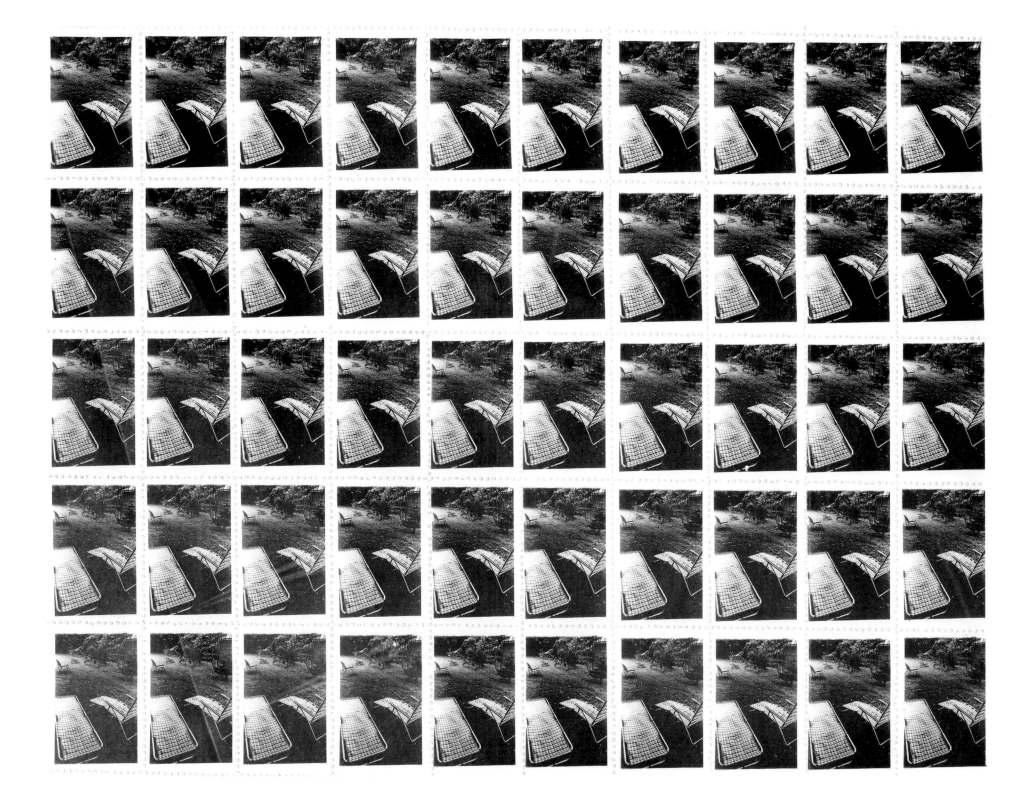

8. *(opposite left)* Variation with Four, *1978, cyanotype with watercolors, 20 x 16.*

9. *(opposite right)* Study for Quadrant, *1979, Diazo print with pastels and felt-tip marker, 1979, 19 1/2 x 15.*

10. Cut Flowers: 6, *1979, lithograph, 16 x 20.*

11. *(right)* Quadrant Variation #2, *1979, cyanotype with watercolors and pastels, 20 x 16.*

Plates 8–11 all from the series Cut Flowers.

12. Hoofbeats, *from the series* B Westerns, *1993, photolithograph with applied Van Dykes, monotype, and pencil, 25 x 36.*

13. Tequila Sunrise, *from the series* B Westerns, *1993, photolithograph with chine collé, monotype, and pencil, 25 1/2 x 36.*

VARIATIONS ON A THEME

Passing Shots
(Mick-a-Matic photographs)

14. *(above) Mick-a-Matic Camera, c. 1969,
10 x 12 x 6.*

Plates 14–30 *all from the series* Passing Shots,
Ektacolor photographs, 15 1/4 x 15 1/4.

15. St. Petersburg, FL (elephant ear), *1975.*

16. *(opposite)* San Diego, CA (polar bear),
1978.

17. (opposite) St. Petersburg, FL (flamingo), *1975.*
18. St. Petersburg, FL (swan tail), *1975.*

(left to right)
19. Maui, HI (palm tree), *1978.*
20. San Diego, CA (eagle head), *1978.*
21. Yellow Flower, Williams's Garden, Sydney, Australia, *1986.*
22. Kangaroo Paws, Perth, Australia, *1986.*

(clockwise from the left)
23. Green Valley, AZ (penny), *1976.*
24. Los Angeles, CA (sidewalk, flowers), *1978.*
25. View of Intersection, Seville, *1983.*
26. Path at Shugakuin Palace, Kyoto, Japan, *1984.*

27. Maui, HI (beach view), *1978*.

28. *(left)* Construction Barrier, Sydney, Australia, *1986.*
29. *(right)* Albuquerque, NM (white horse head), *1978.*

30. *(opposite)* Koi in Sun, Yoyogi Park, Tokyo, Japan, *1984.*

The Lone Ranger
and Tonto

Plates 31–44 from the series Who Was That
Masked Man? I Wanted to Thank Him.

31. Stymied, *1975, Van Dyke with pencil, 22 x 18.*
32. *(opposite left)* Untitled, *1974, gum bichromate*
    with Sanka and pastels, 22 x 18.
33. *(opposite right)* Phantom Stallion, *1974, gum*
    bichromate with Sanka and airbrush, 22 x 18.

Stars Night Variation   *Billy Schenck 1975*

34. *(opposite left)* Starry Night, *1975, cyanotype with watercolors and applied stars, 22 x 18.*

35. *(opposite right)* Untitled, *1977, Van Dyke with watercolors, 22 x 18.*

36. *(left)* New Mexico Sky, *1976, photolithograph, 22 x 18.*

37. *(right)* Starry Night Variation, *1977, photo silkscreen, 22 x 18.*

38. *(opposite left)* In Trouble, *1975, Van Dyke with pastels, 22 x 18.*
39. *(opposite right)* Disillusioned, *1976, Van Dyke with felt-tip marker, 22 x 18.*
40. *(left)* Untitled, *1976, Van Dyke with pastels, 22 x 18.*
41. *(right)* Untitled drawing, *1976, chalk and pencil, 22 x 18.*

There, on a low shelf of rock above the canyon floor a level ray of the disappearing sun illuminated for an instant the tableau of the great white stallion and his gallant rider.

"Hi-Yo, Silver—away!"

42. *(opposite) Details from* Appearance, 1984,
    gelatin silver photographs, 14 x 17 each.
43. New Mexico Sky, 1994, *color Xerox on
    ceramic dinner plate, 11" diameter.*

44. Starry Night, *1994, color Xerox with silver stars and silver bullet on ceramic dinner plate, 11" diameter.*

Flowers

45. Museum Garden, *1973, 12 x 9 gum bichromate*
on 20 x 16 fabric with stitching.

Following pages:
46. *(left)* Dark Garden, *1973, 9 x 13 gum bichromate*
    on 16 x 20 fabric with stitching.
47. *(right)* Greenhouse Portrait (Bea Nettles), *1973, 9 x 13*
    gum bichromate on 16 x 20 fabric with stitching.

48. *(opposite)* Iris Variation #6, *1985, cyanotype
    with watercolors, 20 x 16.*
49. Blue Amaryllis #2, *1987, cyanotype with
    monotype, 24 x 20.*

50. *(opposite left)* White Chrysanthemum #1, *1979, lithograph, 20 x 16.*
51. *(opposite right)* Chrysanthemum with Watermark, *1982, cyanotype with watercolors, 20 x 16.*
52. *(left)* Dark Peony on Gold, *1982, Van Dyke with gouache, 20 x 16.*
53. *(right)* Cut Flower Variation, *1979, Polacolor II photograph, 24 x 20.*

54. *(opposite)* Firecrackers, Madrid Botanical
    Garden, *from the series* Passing Shots,
    *1983, Ektacolor photograph, 15 1/4
    x 15 1/4.*
55. Painted Rose, Alice Springs, Australia,
    from the series Passing Shots, *1986,
    Ektacolor photograph, 15 1/4 x 15 1/4.*

Plates 56–59 *all from the series* Passing Shots, *Ektacolor photographs, 15 1/4 x 15 1/4.*

(clockwise from the left)

56. Hothouse Flowers, Kyoto Botanical Gardens, Kyoto, Japan, *1984.*
57. Tubac, AZ (flowers), *1976.*
58. White Blossoms, Kyoto Botanical Gardens, Kyoto, Japan, *1984.*
59. San Diego, CA (seed pod), *1978.*

60. *(opposite) Frame #11 from* Circumstances of Awakening: Berlin, *1990, from a sequence of eleven photographs, Ektacolor photograph, 19 x 24 each.*

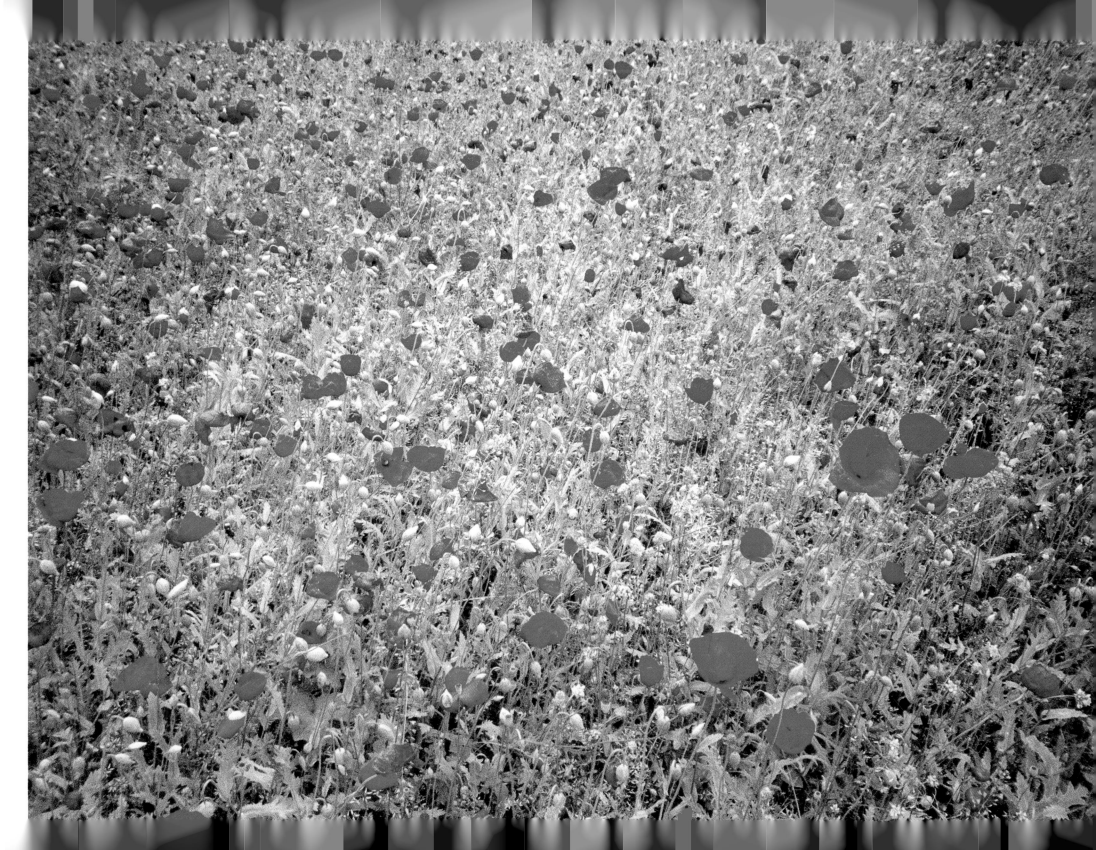

Botanical
Layouts

61. Leaves, *1979, Polacolor II photograph, 24 x 20.*
62. *(opposite left)* Peony I, *1979, Polacolor II
    photograph, 24 x 20.*
63. *(opposite right)* Peony II, *1979, Polacolor II
    photograph, 24 x 20.*

64. *(left)* Amaryllis Belladonna, *1980, Polacolor II photograph, 24 x 20.*
65. *(right)* Stargazer Lily, *1988, Polacolor II photograph, 24 x 20.*

66. *(left)* Calceolaria, *1980, Polacolor II photograph, 24 x 20.*
67. *(right)* Anemone Pavonina, *1980, Polacolor II photograph, 24 x 20.*

68. *(left)* Gladiola, *1988, Polacolor II photograph, 24 x 20.*

69. *(right)* Tulip, *1980, Polacolor II photograph, 24 x 20.*

70. *(opposite)* African Daisy, *1979, Polacolor II photograph, 24 x 20.*

Plate 78

AMBIGUOUS SPACE

71. A Funny Trip #1, *1965, gum bichromate on paper, 15 x 22.*

72. *(opposite)* Steve, Pilot, *1971, gum bichromate on fabric with stitching, 16 x 20.*

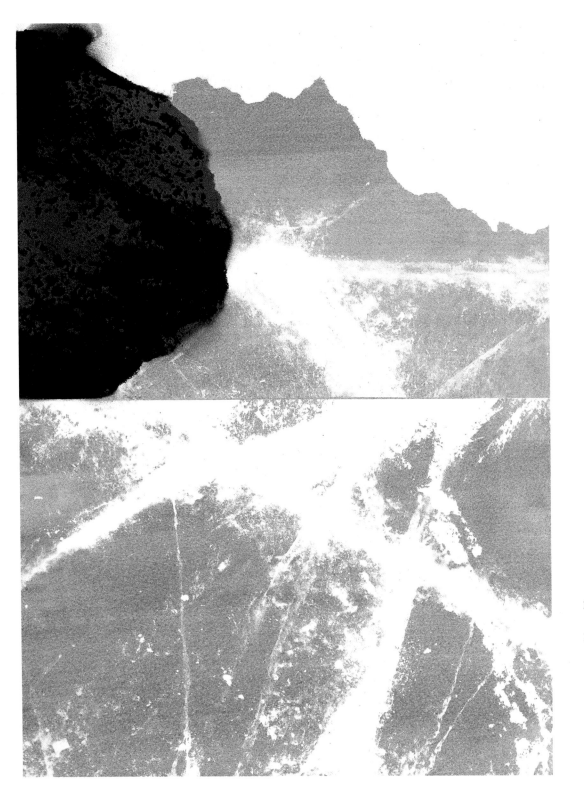

73. No. 5 Silver, *1970, gum bichromate on paper with spray paint stencil, 22 x 14.*

74. *(opposite)* No. 1 Blue, *1970, gum bichromate on paper with spray paint stencil, 16 x 23 1/2.*

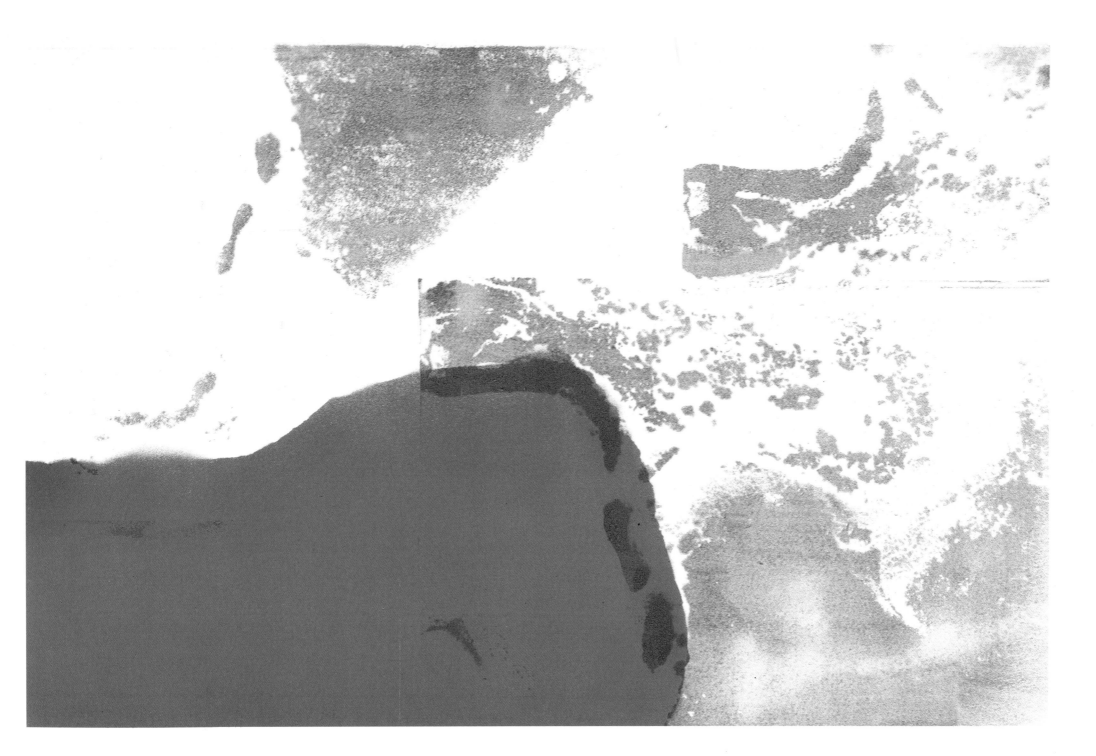

75. *(opposite)* Iris with Red, *1982, Van Dyke with watercolors, 20 x 16.*
76. Ellen II, *1970, gum bichromate on fabric with stitching and appliqué, 20 x 16.*

77. Fish Pond, Garden of Alhambra, Granada, *from the series* Passing Shots, *1983, Ektacolor photograph, 15 1/4 x 15 1/4.*

78. *(opposite)* Cut Flowers: Roses, *1979, Polacolor II photograph, 20 x 24.*

(left to right)
Plates 79–84 from the series Passing Shots,
Ektacolor photographs, 15 1/4 x 15 1/4.

79. Banana Plant in Sunlight, Lisbon, *1983.*
80. Fuschias, Cairns, Australia, *1986.*
81. Grass in Water, Tokyo, Japan, *1984.*
82. Azaleas, Part I, Perth, Australia, *1986.*

83. *(opposite)* San Diego, CA (parrot
    feathers), *1978*.
84. Black and White Composition,
    Lisbon, *1983*.

(opposite) Detail, Ultra Red and Infra Violet,
1967, gum bichromate on paper, 22 x 14 1/2.

COLOR

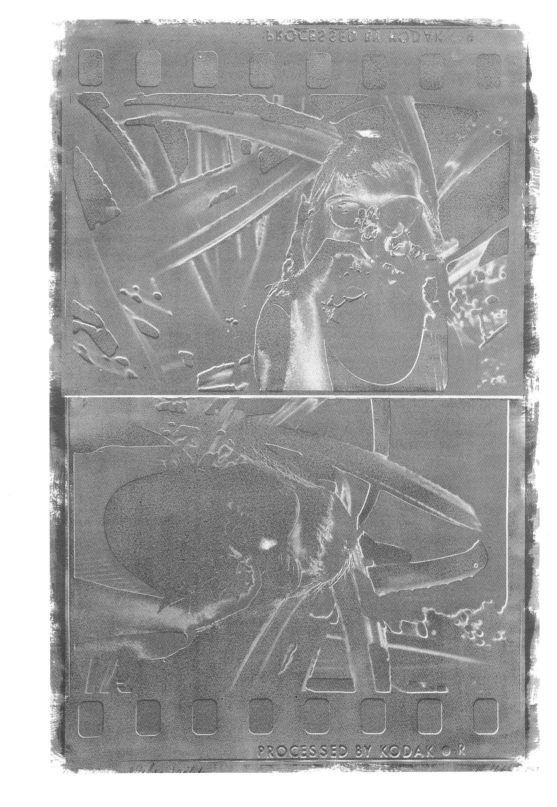

85. *(opposite left)* Someone Else's Snapshot, *1965, woodcut on Japanese
   rice paper, 24 x 18.*
86. *(opposite right)* Ancestors, *1965, woodcut on Japanese rice paper, 24 x 18.*
87. Ultra Red and Infra Violet, *1967, gum bichromate on paper, 22 x 14 1/2.*

88. *(opposite)* Road and Rainbow, *1971, 9 1/2 x 10 3/4*
    gum bichromate on 16 x 20 fabric with stitching.
89. Mejo, Passport Photo, *1971, 10 3/4 x 9 1/2*
    gum bichromate on 16 x 20 fabric with stitching.

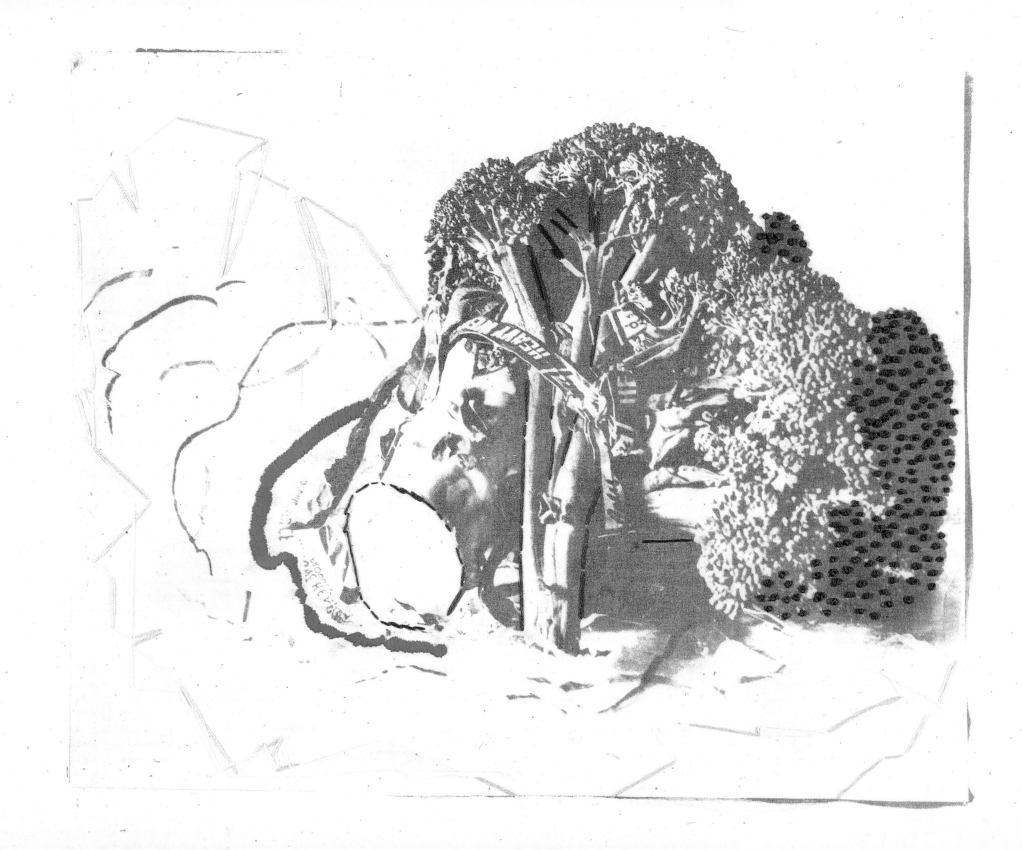

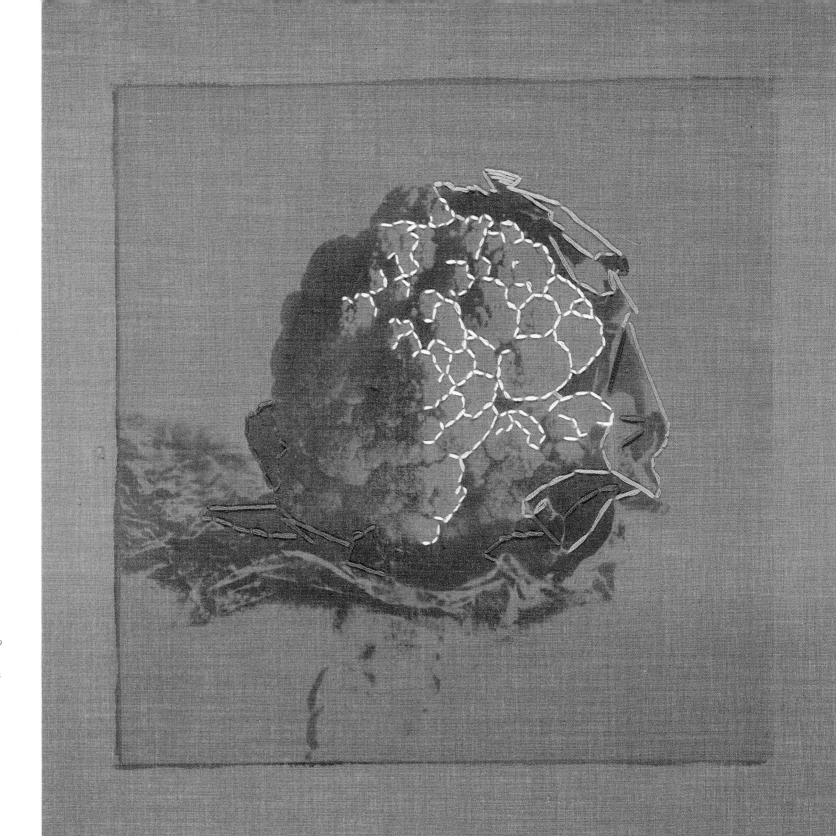

90. *(opposite)* Broccoli, *1972, 9 1/2 x
    10 3/4 gum bichromate on 16 x 20
    fabric with stitching.*
91. Cauliflower, *1972, 10 1/2 x 10 1/2
    gum bichromate on 20 x 16 fabric
    with stitching.*

92. *(opposite)* A Ben Day Day, *1967, gum bichromate on paper, 14 1/2 x 21.*

93. T or C, NM (blue chairs), *from the series* Passing Shots, *1978, Ektacolor photograph, 15 1/4 x 15 1/4.*

94. New Mexico Sky Variation, *from the series* Who Was That Masked
     Man? I Wanted to Thank Him, *1976, photolithograph, 22 x 18.*
95. *(opposite left)* Morning Mum, 1979, *Van Dyke with pastels, 20 x 16.*
96. *(opposite right)* Cut Flower Variation, 1979, *Polacolor II photograph,*
     24 x 20.

97. *(opposite left)* Red Iris, *1985, Van Dyke with watercolors, 20 x 16.*
98. *(opposite right)* Gold Iris, *1985, Van Dyke with watercolors, 20 x 16.*
99. Hot Flower, *1979, Polacolor II photograph, 24 x 20.*

100. *(left)* Fuschias and Chairs, Cairns, Australia, *from the series* Passing Shots, *1986,*
Ektacolor photograph, 15 1/4 x 15 1/4.

101. *(right)* Red Tulips, Kyoto Botanical Gardens, Kyoto, Japan, *from the series*
Passing Shots, *1984, Ektacolor photograph, 15 1/4 x 15 1/4.*

102. *(opposite)* Greenhouse, Waterlilies #11, Kyoto, Japan, *from the series*
Passing Shots, *1984, Ektacolor photograph, 15 1/4 x 15 1/4.*

O. Henry, Thomas Wolfe, Dylan
Thomas and, at one time
or another, every other derelict
drug addict, pimp, whore,
degenerate, pusher, punk-
rock idol, drag queen, con-
artist, ~~drag queen~~ pervert,
shopping bag lady, transvestite,
and dyke that New York has
ever known. The room is

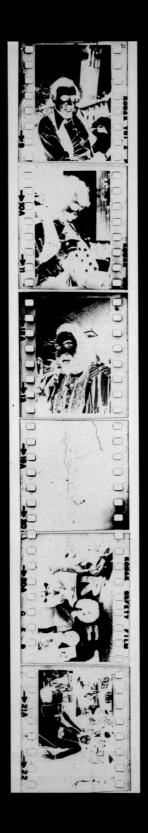

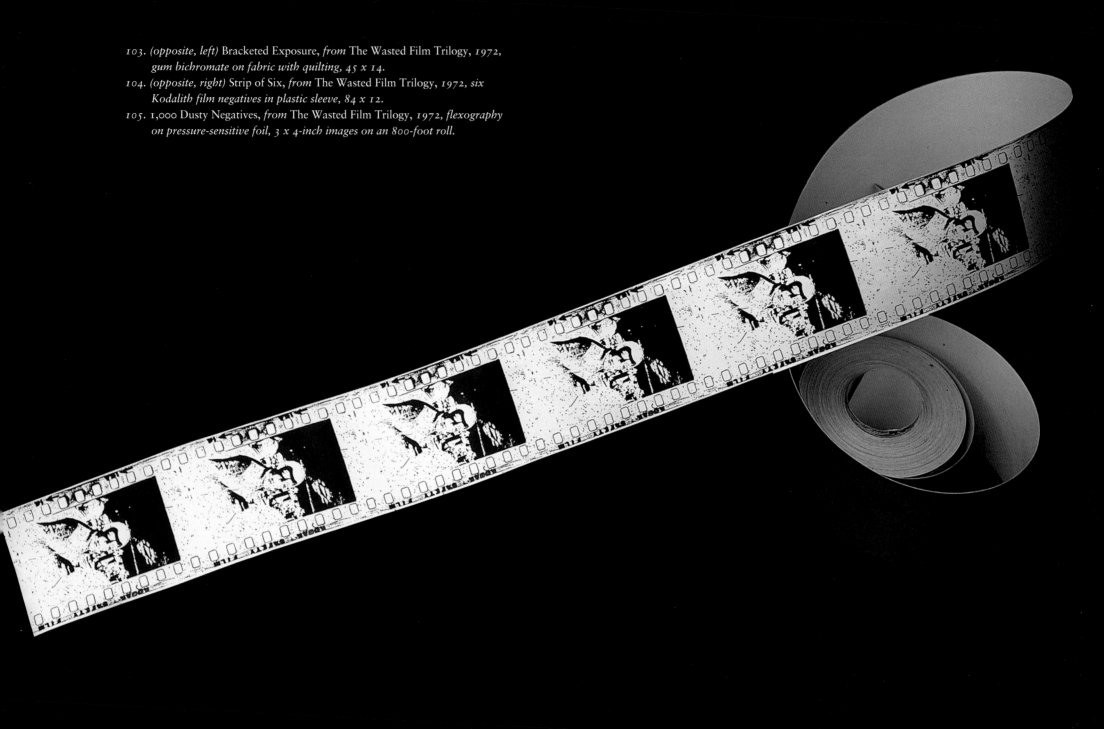

103. *(opposite, left)* Bracketed Exposure, *from* The Wasted Film Trilogy, *1972,*
     gum bichromate on fabric with quilting, 45 x 14.

104. *(opposite, right)* Strip of Six, *from* The Wasted Film Trilogy, *1972, six*
     Kodalith film negatives in plastic sleeve, 84 x 12.

105. 1,000 Dusty Negatives, *from* The Wasted Film Trilogy, *1972, flexography*
     on pressure-sensitive foil, 3 x 4-inch images on an 800-foot roll.

106. Soft Daguerreotype, 1973, Xerox on synthetic
silver fabric in a velvet and satin case, 9 x 24 x 1
(opened, three-dimensional).

HOTEL CHELSEA

WEST TWENTY THIRD STREET
AT SEVENTH AVENUE
NEW YORK, N. Y. 10011
"A LANDMARK OF N.Y.C."

Iuppi
c/o Mable Baca
Chelsea Hotel #628
222 W. 23rd St
NY 10011

NEW YORK, NY
PM
1978

A
US Postage

Betty Hahn
1511 Kit Carson SW
Albuq. NM
87104

"A LANDMARK OF N.Y.C."

1)

HOTEL CHELSEA
New York

AT SEVENTH AVENUE
WEST TWENTY THIRD STREET
NEW YORK, N. Y. 10011

CABLE ADDRESS • HOCHELSEA • NEW YORK
TELEPHONE CHELSEA 3-3700

Dear Betty—

Jan & I are staying at The Chelsea—home to Robert ~~Flaherty~~ Flaherty, O. Henry, Thomas Wolfe, Dylan Thomas and, at one time or another, every other derelict, drug addict, pimp, whore, degenerate, pusher, punk-rock idol, drag queen, con-artist, ~~drag queen~~ pervert, shopping bag lady, transvestite, and dyke that New York has ever known. The room is as sleezy, if not more so, than the clientelle. We like it.

Did you realize that NY has been invaded by

LARGE and SOUND-PROOF ROOMS

107. *(opposite left) Envelope from* Letter from the Chelsea Hotel, *1979, photo silkscreen, 30 1/4 x 21 1/4.*

108. *(opposite right) Page 1 from* Letter from the Chelsea Hotel, *1979, photo silkscreen, 30 1/4 x 21 1/4.*

109. *T-shirt from* Letter from the Chelsea Hotel, *1979, photo silkscreen, size S, M, or L.*

ART REMOVAL SQUAD

*Essential preparation for all artists who aspire to CONTROL of their own artworks
...hundreds of classified test questions complete with illustrations--*

1. Although there are innumerable crimes each year which require the concentrated activity and most skillful ingenuity of the ART REMOVAL SQUAD, certain patterns lessen the burden of classification
   (A) confusion of ownership with consignment
   (B) taste lapse, relapse, collapse
   (C) art held hostage through ejectment
   (D) financial fantasy (the phantom buyer)
   (E) illusion vs. reality (the phantom publication)
   (F) things about to disappear
   (G) art held hostage through contributory negligence

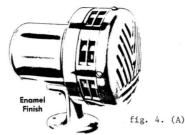

¡NO, DIOS NO...!

fig. 1. (G)

2. It is of primary importance in art reconnaissance to
   (A) have the current exhibit under surveillance
   (B) ascertain peculiar habits of occupants
   (C) have knowledge of possible counterattack
   (D) identify avenues of approach
   (E) have visual intelligence gathering
   (F) specify The Removal

fig. 2. (D)

fig. 3. (F)

fig. 3. (C)

3. The Removal Commander, when considering members for the Removal party, should look for qualities of
   (A) enhanced capacity   (D) experience in DMZ
   (B) not easily excited   (E) mental mobility
   (C) small feet   (F) Hidden Danger

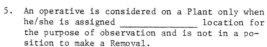

Enamel Finish

fig. 4. (A)

4. In conducting a raid on the offending premises, the element of surprize is <u>most</u> important. The best control method to insure coordinated action that will lead to this end is
   (A) radio communication   (D) hand signals
   (B) rapidograph drawings   (E) Polaroid
   (C) whistle signals   (F) time coordination

fig. 5. (C)

5. An operative is considered on a Plant only when he/she is assigned _____ location for the purpose of observation and is not in a position to make a Removal.
   (A) an indefinite   (D) a critical
   (B) a definite   (E) a gallery
   (C) a disguise as a buyer (F) framing on

6. When considered necessary, <u>all</u> members of the Removal Squad should be equipped with
   (A) sneakers   (D) a large unmarked vehicle
   (B) dark suit
   (C) Hawaiian shirt   (E) insult-proof vest
   (F) smoke pot   (F) darkest glasses

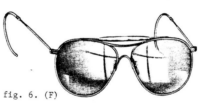

fig. 6. (F)

fig. 6. (D)

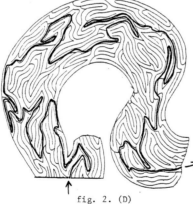

fig. 6. (E)

fig. 3. (B)

There's a Thrill in Bringing a Crook to Justice Through Scientific **CRIME DETECTION**

art scene of the crime productions

110. *(opposite)* The Art Removal Squad, *1980, Xerox on card stock,*
11 x 8 1/2 (front and back).

111. Chicago Family: Aunt, *1979, Polacolor II photograph, 24 x 20.*

112. *(following pages)* Teddy Bear (front) and (back),
1988, Polacolor II photographs, 20 x 24.

Teddybär als Container sowie andere Gegenstände mit einge-
bauter Spionagekamera, die Agenten vom US-Geheimdienst er-
hielten.

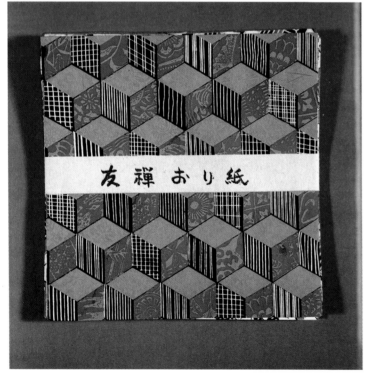

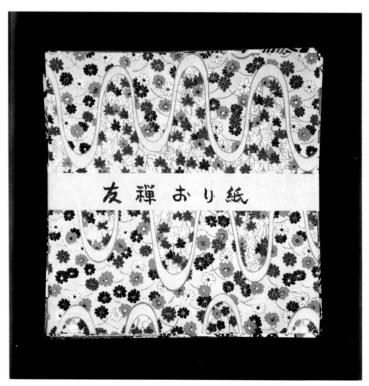

113. A Japanese Collage in 5 Parts, 1988, five Polacolor II photographs, 24 x 20 each.

友禅おり紙

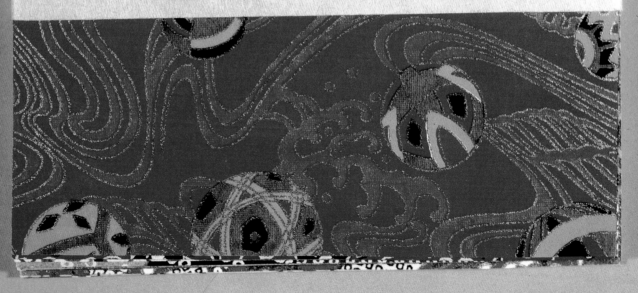

CINEMATIC AND NARRATIVE SEQUENCES

114. *(these and following pages)* Shinjuku, 1984,
sequence of eleven Ektacolor photographs, 17 x 24 each.

Last night I dreamed

I went to Tokyo again.

I thought I saw

forbidden colors

in the neon of Shinjuku...

Did someone try to warn me?

In what language?

I can't remember.

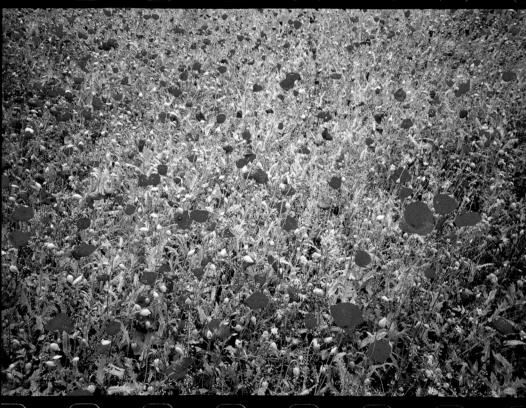

116. *(following pages)* A Case of XX, *1981, ten gelatin silver photographs (from a sequence of thirty-three), 11 x 11 each.*

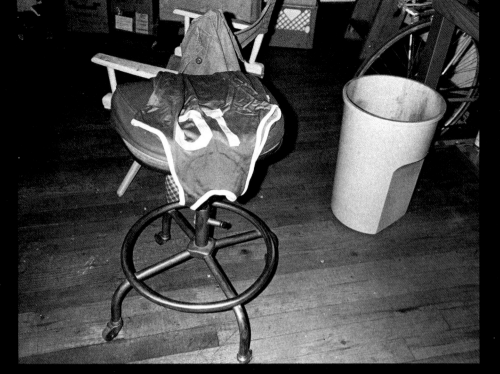

To a private detective, it was the most familiar of all sordid stories. *You are assigned to investigate a crime scene in a building. The first thing you should search for evidence and then photograph is*
(A) walls   *(B) ceiling*
(C) floor   *(D) furniture*
(E) light fixtures

I got a cigarette out and went through the elaborately slow motions of lighting it. *To recognize evidence of crime the investigator must first know the conditions at the scene of the crime. The scene of crime may reveal clues as to the manner in which the crime was committed and the movements of the perpetrator.*

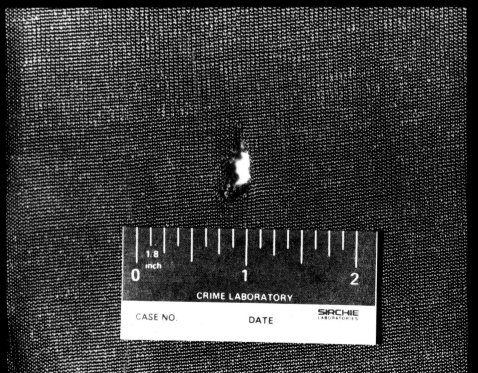

INCIDENT OR CRIME

REC'D BY

FROM

TIME

DATE

The apartment wasn't much, but it was home. It seemed as if I'd been gone a year. You cleaned up this morning, I told myself. So what? Make that yesterday morning. But I hadn't cleaned up. *The contents of all articles of
furniture and containers, such as wastebaskets and
cuspidors, should be carefully noted, and letters and
memoranda read and listed in the investigators' notes.
Care should be exercised in handling any papers which
may bear latent fingerprints.* Aside from that it was a
dead world, without sound, almost without color.

118. Collect from Berlin, *1991, sequence of four photolithographs, 27 x 36 each.*

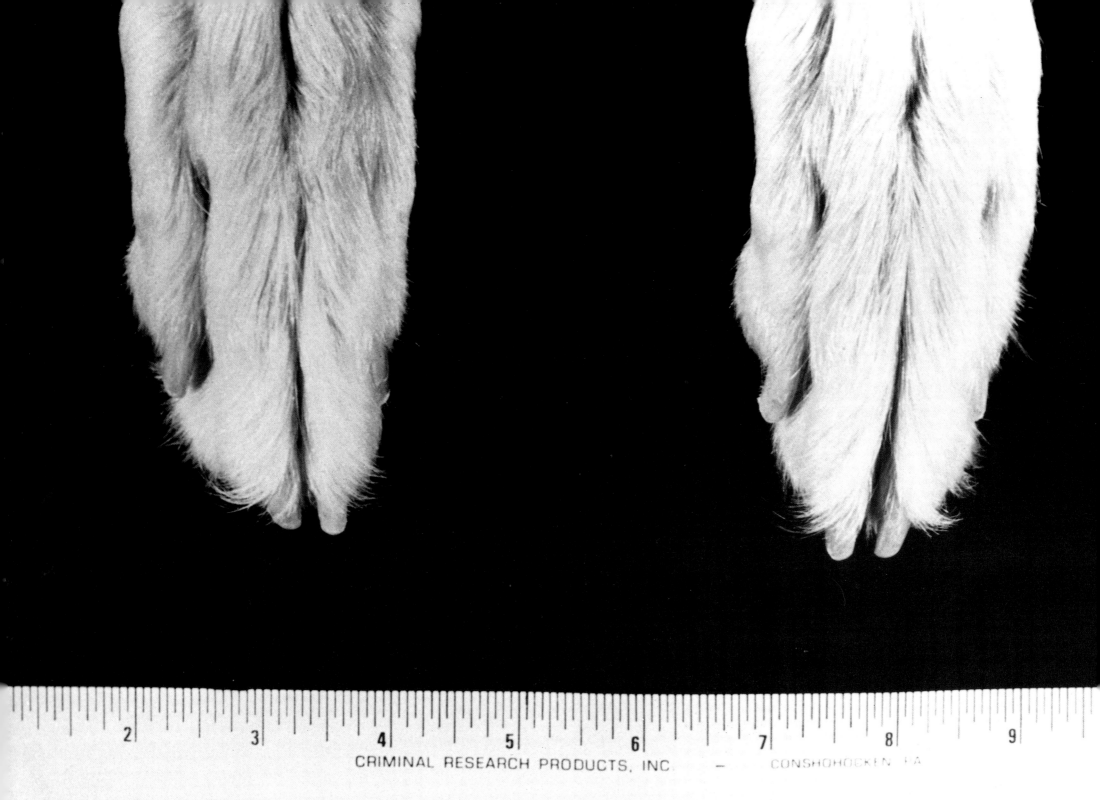

CRIMINAL RESEARCH PRODUCTS, INC.   —   CONSHOHOCKEN, PA

THE PHOTOGRAPHIC WORK OF BETTY HAHN 1964–1994

MICHELE M. PENHALL

(opposite) Detail from Crime in the Home, Exhibit J: Suspect in Fingerprint Lab, *1982 (original in color), Cibachrome, 11 x 14.*

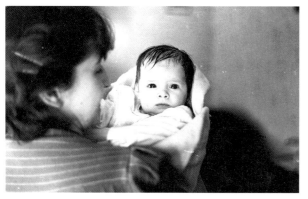

Age five weeks, 1940.
Photograph by Eugene Okon.

First Holy Communion portrait, 1946.
Photograph by Jack Braschel.

1940

Elizabeth Jean Okon is born on 11 October at 4:58 P.M. at Loretto Hospital, Chicago, Illinois. She is the first of four children of Eugene and Esther Okon. Eugene Okon works as a United States customs officer.

1946–49

She attends grades 1 through 4 at Our Lady of Victory Catholic School, Chicago, Illinois.

1950

An aunt, Marcella Brown, gives Betty her first camera, a Brownie #2.

Children's Playmate Magazine publishes Betty's drawing of two horses, and she receives some 200 fan letters as a result.

1950–53

The Okon family moves to Indianapolis, Indiana; Betty attends grades 5 through 7 at Westfield public school.

1954

She attends and graduates from the 8th grade at Immaculate Heart Catholic School, Indianapolis, Indiana.

Her interest in mystery novels begins—she reads Sir Arthur Conan Doyle's *The Complete Sherlock Holmes.*

1954–55

She attends 9th grade at Carmel High School, Carmel, Indiana.

1955–58

Elizabeth attends and graduates from Scecina Memorial Catholic High School, Indianapolis, Indiana.

Watercolor entry in the 1957 National Scholastic Art Contest, for which Betty Hahn received a Hallmark Honor prize and a $100 purchase award.

1957

She receives a Hallmark Honor Prize in the National Scholastic Art Awards Competition for high school students, a $100 purchase award for a watercolor now on permanent display at Hallmark Cards, Inc., Kansas City, Missouri.

1958

She enters Indiana University in Bloomington, Indiana, with a four-year scholarship and majors in fine arts. Here she meets Henry Holmes Smith, who serves as her undergraduate advisor for four years. She studies art history with Henry Hope and Albert Elsen, design with George Sadek, and printmaking with Rudy Pozzatti.

1961

During her junior year in college she takes her first course from Smith.

1962

On 27 October she marries Alan J. Hahn at Holy Spirit Catholic Church in Indianapolis. The couple obtains a Mexican divorce in 1968.

(left) *Photograph published in the* Indiana Star *(September 23, 1962) announcing Betty's engagement to Alan Hahn.*

(right) *Photography students with Henry Holmes Smith, Indiana University, 1964. Front row: John Crowley (center), others unknown. Back row, left to right: Smith, Frank Wagner, Robert Fichter, Betty Hahn, Lance Bird. Photograph by Frank Wagner.*

1963

Hahn graduates with a Bachelor of Arts degree from Indiana University and begins her graduate studies there where she meets Robert Fichter, David Haberstich, and Gayle Smalley, who came to study with Henry Holmes Smith.

She works part-time for Smith in the department's photography lab.

1964

She begins a two-year graduate assistantship with Henry Holmes Smith.

1965

In October, at the suggestion of Smith, Hahn begins experimenting with the gum bichromate process.

1966

Betty Hahn graduates with a Master of Fine Arts degree from Indiana University.

She moves to Ithaca, New York, and works at Cornell University, making slides for the Art History Department slide library.

1967

Hahn moves to Rochester, New York, and works as a social worker for two years while continuing to make gum prints.

In Rochester she meets Tom Barrow, Roger Mertin, Bea Nettles,

Betty Hahn in her office at the Rochester Institute of Technology, 1972.

Keith Smith, James Borcoman, Nathan and Joan Lyons. She also meets Daniel Andrews, an engineer working for Kodak.

She participates in Nathan Lyons's 1967–68 Visual Studies Workshop.

1969
She begins teaching photography and design to deaf students at the National Technical Institute for the Deaf, Rochester Institute of Technology.

1970
On 26 March she marries Daniel Andrews.

Hahn meets Tom Muir Wilson and John Pfahl. She transfers to the School of Photographic Arts and Sciences at RIT and teaches there until 1975. She travels to England, Holland, Switzerland, and Paris.

1972
She meets Lee Witkin at a reception at the George Eastman House in Rochester, New York.

1973
Her first one-person show, *Betty Hahn,* opens in New York City at the Witkin Gallery.

She travels to Bloomington, Indiana, to interview Henry Holmes Smith for an article commissioned by *Image* magazine.

1974
She receives a grant from the National Endowment for the Arts to be a visiting artist at Franconia College, Franconia, New Hampshire, to continue projects in nonsilver processes and mixed media. While at Franconia she works with Eileen Cowin, Robert Fichter, Ellen Brooks, and Darryl Curran.

Hahn executes the first works which focus on the Lone Ranger. This subject recurs throughout her work into 1994.

Hahn visits Mexico and Canada and lectures at A Space Gallery in Toronto.

She meets Anne Noggle and Margery Mann who are organizing the exhibition and publication *Women of Photography.*

1975
She receives a grant from the New York State Council on the Arts to continue her work with nonsilver processes.

Hahn receives as a gift from Phil Condax, curator of equipment at the George Eastman House, a Mick-a-Matic toy camera, and she begins the "Passing Shots" series, which continues through 1986.

1976
In January, Betty Hahn is hired by Van Deren Coke as a visiting professor to teach photography at the University of New Mexico in Albuquerque. In August she accepts a full-time position as an associate professor with tenure.

She does her first lithographs, *New Mexico Sky,* with Bill Lyman III in Albuquerque, New Mexico.

Hahn meets photography dealer Andrew Smith, who later represents her.

1977
Hahn travels to Canada and lectures at Ryerson Polytechnic in Toronto.

She receives a Research Allocation Grant from the University of New Mexico to work on the Kallitype process.

As a visiting artist at Tamarind Institute working on the *Cut Flower* series, Hahn experiments with collotypes and other photolithographic processes.

(left) Albuquerque, New Mexico, 1982, left to right: Bill Lucas, Antonella Russo, Beaumont Newhall, Ralph Steiner, Betty Hahn.

(right) Traveling in Spain, 1983. Photograph by Gadi Gofbarg.

1978
Hahn receives her first grant from the National Endowment for the Arts for ongoing projects.

She travels to Hawai'i and begins photographing themes of crime, mystery, and intrigue.

She meets Detective Ron Pincomb at the Indiana University Alumni dinner held at the Albuquerque Hilton Hotel. He provides Hahn with criminal investigation products catalogues as well as technical information regarding crimes scenes and evidence procedures.

1979
Hahn travels to Cambridge, Massachusetts, to work for the first time on the 20 x 24 Polaroid camera. Her first Polaroids result in *Chicago Family*, the first *Botanical Layouts*, and some double-exposed flowers. She collaborates in the studio with Robert Fichter.

She works with Jim Kraft of Unified Arts, Robert Fichter, and Darryl Curran on the *Chelsea Letter* project.

Hahn is again a visiting artist at Tamarind Institute for the *Cut Flowers* series, and she also completes the *Botanical Layout: Peony* lithograph edition.

1981
She travels to Austria and lectures at the Hochschule für Angewandte Kunst in Vienna.

1983
Hahn receives her second National Endowment for the Arts grant to continue the *Passing Shots* project and crime/mystery sequences.

She travels to Spain and lectures at the Universidad de Barcelona, and L'Institut D'Estudis Fotográfics de Catalunya, both in Barcelona. She meets Joan Fontcuberta and starts work on exhibition and publication *Contemporary Spanish Photography*.

1984
She travels to Japan to lecture and conduct workshops at the Kyoto Art Institute in Kyoto, and the Belca House in Shizuhara.

Certificate for completing the Evidence Photography course at the University of Southern California, 1984.

With Anne Noggle she travels to Fiji, Tasmania, New Zealand, and Australia and lectures at the Sydney College of Arts, the Australian Center of Photography in Sydney, and the Experimental Art Foundation in Adelaide.

1987
In May, the artist's husband, Daniel Andrews, dies.

Hahn receives a fellowship from the Visual Arts Research Institute at Arizona State University in Tempe. In November she travels to Tempe and executes the *Landscape with Cloud Variations* project.

1988
She receives a grant from Polaroid and works on *A Japanese Paper Collage in 5 Parts, Man Coming into Focus, Teddy Bear,* and an additional four *Botanical Layouts.*

1990
Hahn travels with Charles McClelland to Czechoslovakia, Germany, and Poland, and lectures at the Institute of Art History, Jagiellonian University, Krakow, Poland. With Rodney Hamon she works on *Circumstances of Awakening* and *Collect from Berlin.*

In November she attends a two-day seminar for the advancement of Forensic Evidence Photography and is the guest speaker at the annual banquet for the Evidence Photographer's International Council, held this year in Albuquerque, New Mexico.

1991
She collaborates with Rodney Hamon of Black and Blue Press on the *B-Westerns* project.

1992
She travels again with McClelland to Germany and Switzerland and for the first time to Italy, where they visit Florence, Siena, Pisa, and Bologna.

While in Japan she meets Eikoh Hosoe and Yasu Suzuka and makes images for the Shinjuku series.

Hahn receives the Honored Educator award from the Society for Photographic Education.

She joins the Evidence Photographer's International Council (EPIC) and attends an EPIC seminar in forensic photography at the University of Southern California in Los Angeles.

1985
Hahn returns to Japan for another lecture and workshop at the Photohouse in Kyoto. She visits Spain again to finish work on *Contemporary Spanish Photography* and also travels to China and Hong Kong.

1986
During the spring semester Betty Hahn is made full professor at the University of New Mexico.

(left) Junior prom rephotographic survey portrait with Jim Rupp, June 1957 and June 1989. Photographs by Eugene Okon.

(right) Albuquerque, New Mexico, 1992. Photograph by Charles Rushton.

1993
She receives a grant from the College of Fine Arts at the University of New Mexico and continues work on *B-Westerns* with Rodney Hamon.

1995
In November, *Betty Hahn: Photography or Maybe Not*, a thirty-year retrospective opens at the Museum of Fine Arts in Santa Fe, New Mexico.

CATALOGUE OF WORKS

THE PROJECTS IN THIS CATALOGUE represent Betty Hahn's work from 1964 through June 1994. Before her untimely death in 1993, Roberta DeGolyer gathered the preliminary technical material for many projects, and I am grateful for her work. Every attempt has been made to provide as much accurate information as possible. I am indebted to Betty Hahn for sharing so much material and so many hours with me and for granting me liberal access to her library and archive.

Each catalogue entry includes the project title, a brief, annotated description of the work, a list of materials used, technical information, and titles of individual works, when known. Some of the individual works are followed by one or two sets of parentheses. The letters in the first set refer to the public or the first private collection where the work exists outside of the artist's collection (see the Collections list). Those individuals who wish to remain anonymous are named only in the general collections list. The figure in the second set indicates the number of additional unique prints or editions made, when known. Standard photographic dimensions such as 35mm and 4 x 5 are used throughout where relevant. Other dimensions refer to paper or fabric size only; height precedes width and inches precede centimeters. Unless noted otherwise, all works were printed by the artist.

178

Someone Else's Snapshot #2.

PROJECT 1

WOODCUTS 1964, 1967

Woodcut prints made from white pine and discarded drawing boards. The images are from family snapshots, other found photographs, and one nineteenth-century daguerreotype and one tintype.

18 x 24, 45.72 x 60.96
1, 2, 3, 4, and 5 colors: red, yellow, green, black, grey
Printed on Japanese rice paper
Printed by Will Werblow

Titles:
Ancestors (ALH) (8); variant *Girl in a Red Coat Daguerreotype* (8)
Family (after Degas' Bellelli Family) (PLC, CJS) (7)
Family Group (8)
Five Informants (ALH) (8)
Matriarchy (ALH) (8)

Someone Else's Snapshot (7)
Someone Else's Snapshot #2 (RJO) (8)
Zoological Landscape (CJS) (8)

Alice in the Presence of Palominos.

PROJECT 2

GUM BICHROMATES ON PAPER 1965–70

Gum bichromate prints from 35mm and 120 roll film negatives that were enlarged onto graphic arts film and then contact printed. Some prints have applied watercolors and/or fluorescent spray paint. Most are unique pieces, but some images have been printed more than once.

All works are approximately 15 x 22, 38.1 x 55.88 unless noted otherwise.
Each image is printed in a variety of colors including but not limited to: green, blue, brown, violet, indigo, yellow, red, orange, lampblack, gold, and silver.
Printed on Rives BFK, Arches, and Fabriano

Titles:

1965

Seasonal Landscape Transition (RH)
Variant; Multiple Landscape #2 (IMP)
A Funny Trip #1
Robert Beside Himself
*A Funny Trip #2; variant A Funny Trip Back
   and Forth* (IMP) 14 1/2 x 21 1/2, 36.83 x 54.61
My Sisters—Negative and Positive (IMP)

1966

He Did it Again
Warrior I

1967

Warrior II
Bather, A Senseless Duplication (NGC)
A Ben Day Day (IMP) 14 1/2 x 21, 36.83 x 53.34
A Ben Day Day # 2
Ultra Red and Infra Violet (NGC) 22 x 14 1/2,
   55.88 x 36.83
Classic Solution I 14 1/2 x 21 1/2, 36.83 x 54.61

1968

Inner Rainbow (EEO, IMP, NGC)
Seasonal Rainbow Transition (LTB)
Middle Eye
TV Failure (NGC) 14 1/2 x 22, 36.83 x 55.88
Ballroom
Upper Green
Processed by Kodak (NGC, IMP) 15 x 22 1/2,
   38.1 x 57.15
Girl by Four Highways; variant Girl by Four Roads
   (NGC, IMP)
Metallic Reversal
Parking Lot; variant A Lot of Parking 21 1/2 x 14,
   54.61 x 35.56
Red and Blue Sisters; variant Red and Blue Daughters
Kodak Tri-X Pan Film (NGC) 22 1/2 x 15
Alice in the Presence of Palominos 22 x 14 3/4,
   55.88 x 37.46

1969

Dan Four Times (NGC)
Cathy Grant (NGC)
Untitled (TV) 18 x 22, 45.72 x 30.48
D., M., and A. (IMP)

1970

No. 1 Blue
No. 2 Brown and Silver—destroyed
No. 3 Cerise Red (BN)
No. 4 Black
No. 5 Silver (NGC)
No. 6 Silver

Red Barn.

PROJECT 3

GUM BICHROMATES ON FABRIC 1970–73

Gum bichromate prints from 35mm and 120 roll film
negatives, enlarged onto graphic arts film and then
contact printed. All works are embellished with different colored embroidery thread. Subjects for these
prints include portraits, landscapes, gardens, architecture, television images, fruits, and vegetables.

16 x 20, 40.64 x 50.8 with individual image sizes that
range from 9 1/2 x 9 1/2, 24.13 x 24.13 to 10 3/4 x
14, 27.30 x 35.56.
Each image is printed in one color including but not

limited to: lampblack, brown, blue, silver, orange,
and green.
Printed on unbleached cotton and colored cotton
blend fabrics.
Most are unique pieces but some images, as noted,
have been printed more than once.

Titles:

1970

Dan, Passport Photo
Betty, Passport Photo (VM)
Ellen I
Ellen II
People Walking under Rainbow (LTB)
Kent Family (PLC)
Untitled (Eastman House) (IMP)
Roger and Joni (RJM, NGC, IMP)
Christmas 1970
For Aaron (JES)

1971

Judy, Passport Photo
Mejo, Passport Photo
Ellen III
Portrait: L.K. (Les Krims) (2)
Barbara—Genessee Park (MNM) (2)
Dover Park Family—2
(Untitled) London Street
Road and Rainbow (JMSS, SPA, NGC,
   IMP, CAP) (10)
Color TV Failure
Railroad Crossing
White Barn
Red Barn (NGC)
Steve; Pilot

1972

Julie and Dan
Terraced Garden (JP, BI)
Broccoli (BI, IMP) (2)
Red Cabbage (BI)
Grapefruit (BI) (2)

Cabbage (NGC) (2)
Lettuce (NGC) (2)
Cauliflower

1973

Museum Garden (RSB)
Dark Garden (GR, UNM)
Secret Garden (ADF)
Green Landscape (NGC)
Bloom's Tree
Tulips
Cloudy Sky
The Gray Fence (IMP)
Red Building
Roberts Drive Family (EEO)
Family in Park
Portrait: Miss N.
Greenhouse Portrait (Bea Nettles) (ANE, UNM)
Garden Portrait (Lani Czyzewski) (NGC)
Bristol Garden

PROJECT 4

MINIATURE GUM BICHROMATES 1971

These are gum bichromate contact prints from 120 black and white roll-film negatives. Each image shows a nude female torso holding a fruit or vegetable, and the color of each print corresponds with the color of the fruit or vegetable held by the figure.

2 x 2, 5.08 x 5.08
Printed on Rives paper
16 photographs in series, edition not to exceed 10

Titles:

Cauliflower (NGC) (4)
Zucchini (BN,GR, NGC) (7)
Watermelon (NGC) (3)
Eggplant (JB, RAS, UNM) (4)
Eggplant II (NGC) (4)
Red Cabbage (NGC) (5)
White Scallops (NGC) (8)

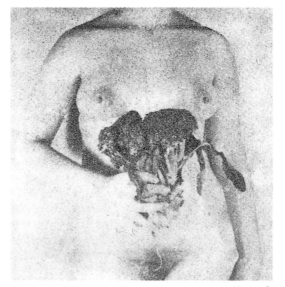

Broccoli.

Broccoli (NGC, WLS) (8)
Broccoli II (8)
Sweet Potatoes (NGC) (5 artist's proofs)
Bananas (JB, NGC) (5)
Purple Onions (GR, NGC) (4 artist's proofs)
Grapefruit (NGC) (5 artist's proofs)
Grapefruit II (10)
Grapefruit III (10)
Cabbage (NGC) (unnumbered)

PROJECT 5

COMMEMORATIVES 1971

Gelatin silver photographs from 35mm negatives, commercially printed and perforated. Each image is reduced to approximately the size of a postage stamp, with fifty examples printed per sheet of 8 x 10 paper. The entire sheet is perforated much like a commercial sheet of stamps. An undetermined but small number of images also exist as 3M Color-in-Color photocopies in magenta, cerise, green, red, and blue, but these are not perforated. These photographs depict or commemorate various minor events in the artist's life during 1971, such as a friend's wedding, a trip from

Untitled.

Rochester to a Florida beach, and a performance piece staged by Linda Montano.

8 x 10, 20.32 x 25.4
20 photographs in series
1 complete set of each different image

Titles:

Airmail Stamp
Kitchen
Mendon Pond
Nathan
Sharon's Wedding
Ten Cent Stamp
Park
Untitled (13)
Les Krims
RWF, Vero Beach
Volkswagon
Garden
Adam
Rodeo
Front

PROJECT 6

(See Plates 103–5)

THE WASTED FILM TRILOGY 1972

All images in this project are from 35mm negatives. These photographs were made at the "Market Diner Bash," a party organized by A. D. Coleman and Neal Slavin and held at the Market Diner, 572 Eleventh Avenue, in New York. Photographs by the artist and other photographers who attended this party were later exhibited at the Underground Gallery in New York from June through August of 1972.

1,000 Dusty Negatives (original roll LP, LTB, RAS; modern roll MNM)
3 x 4-inch images on an 800-foot roll
This is a roll of pressure-sensitive foil tape with a reversed negative portrait of Lee Witkin printed in black ink. The same image is repeated throughout the entire roll.

Bracketed Exposure (MNM)
45 x 14, 114.3 x 35.56
In this three-dimensional work a portrait of Lee Witkin is reprinted in black gum bichromate on three continuous panels that measure 14 x 15, 35.56 x 38.1 each. The panels are unbleached cotton fabric and have added machine stitching and padding.

Strip of Six (MNM)
84 x 12, 213.36 x 30.48
This work includes six portraits of different photographers on one strip of graphic arts film encased in a plastic sleeve.

PROJECT 7

(See Plate 106)

DAGUERREOTYPE MESSAGES TO THE PAST 1973

These images are Xeroxed on synthetic silver fabric and sewn into fabricated daguerreotype display cases. The cases are constructed from wood and covered with materials that include red velvet and gold brocade rickrack. Inspired by nineteenth-century daguerreotypes and Claes Oldenburg's oversized soft sculptures, images for the soft daguerreotypes include nudes and landscapes made in New York state.

9 x 12 x 2, 22.86 x 30.48 x 5.08
8 images each in a separate case

Titles:

Soft Daguerreotype (IMP)
For H. D. T.
For P. H. E.
Untitled (5)

PROJECT 8

LONE RANGER SERIES 1974–79

This project includes cyanotypes, Van Dykes, gum bichromates, duotones, photo silkscreens, and lithographs made from a Hollywood still photograph of the Lone Ranger and Tonto each sitting on a horse in a desert landscape in Tucson, Arizona. The image is punctuated by a saguaro cactus that rises up behind the Lone Ranger. The artist found this photograph in a stationery store and has used it throughout all of her Lone Ranger projects. Applied materials for the unique works on paper and fabric include watercolor, graphite, pastels, felt-tip marker, silver paper stars, and Sanka instant coffee. All works, including editions, are 22 x 18 unless noted otherwise.

22 x 18, 55.88 x 45.72
Cyanotypes on paper (DDC, ML, MO, BL, UNM) (22)

L.R. #29.

Van Dykes on paper (MLS, SR) (29)
Gum bichromates on paper (JMY, CAM) (5)
Van Dykes on white cotton with appliqué (RH)
Printed on Rives, Fabriano Classico, and charcoal paper

The series title is *Who Was That Masked Man? I Wanted To Thank Him.* Individual works include:

Stymied
In Trouble
Disillusioned
Disguised
Starry Night
Phantom Stallion

Print editions:
Phantom Stallion 1974 (RH, GR)
Duotone
8 1/2 x 11 1/2, 21.59 x 27.94
Edition of 50
Printed on AB Dick offset copy paper by Joe Ruther, Franconia, New Hampshire

Phantom Stallion 1976 (AN, JKJB, AT, CCP)
Photo silkscreen
11 x 14, 27.94 x 35.56
Edition of 125
10 artist's proofs
2 colors: brown, beige
Printed on Superfine Cover by Vistec Graphics, Ltd.,
Rochester, New York

This print was included in the *New Mexico Portfolio*,
a portfolio of 25 works by photographers living in
New Mexico. The limited edition portfolio was pub-
lished by the Center of the Eye Collaborative, Santa
Fe, New Mexico, produced by Andrew Smith and
Paige Pinnell. The portfolio director was Alex Traube.

New Mexico Sky 1976 (GR, IMP, NGC, SFM)
Photolithograph
2 colors: grey, blue blend
Printed on Rives
Edition of 15
1 artist's proof
Printed by Bill Lyman III, Sandstone Graphics,
Albuquerque, New Mexico

New Mexico Sky Variation 1976
Photolithograph
2 colors: brown, rainbow blend
Printed on Rives
Edition of 15
1 artist's proof
Printed by Bill Lyman III, Sandstone Graphics,
Albuquerque, New Mexico

New Mexico Sky (variations) 1976 (PLB, NASS)
Photolithograph with applied watercolor and/or
pastels
1 color: brown
Printed on Rives
10 prints each with applied watercolor and/or pastels
Printed by Bill Lyman III, Sandstone Graphics,
Albuquerque, New Mexico

Starry Night Variation #2 1977 (DDM, JKJB, JP,
MNM, NGC)
Photo silkscreen
4 colors: brown, grey, blue, silver
Printed on Arches 88
Edition of 14
1 artist's proof
Printed by Jim Kraft, Unified Arts, Albuquerque,
New Mexico

L.R. # 29 1977 (JP, LL, MNM)
Photo silkscreen
1 color: blue
Printed on Rives
Edition of 25
Bon à tirer
2 record impressions
Printed by Harry Westlund, Serigraphics,
Albuquerque, New Mexico

L.R. # 30 1977 (UNM, MNM)
Photo silkscreen
1 color: brown
Printed on Rives BFK
Edition of 30
Bon à tirer
3 trial proofs
2 record impressions
Printed by Harry Westlund, Serigraphics,
Albuquerque, New Mexico

Taos Sky 1979 (RH)
Lithograph
2 colors: brown, rainbow roll
Printed on Somerset Textured
Edition of 35
Bon à tirer
Unknown number of artist's proofs
Printed by Bill Lyman III, Sandstone Graphics,
Rochester, New York

Seaneck Views.

PROJECT 9

POSTCARDS 1974

These Van Dyke photographs or cyanotypes with applied watercolors depict motel scenes in New Hampshire and are printed on one sheet of paper, then folded accordion-style to simulate packaged tourist views.
This project was made possible by a grant from the
National Endowment for the Arts while Hahn was a
visiting artist at Franconia College, Franconia, New
Hampshire.

29 1/2 x 6 1/4, 74.93 x 15.87
8 images
Printed on Rives and Rives BFK

Title:

Seaneck Views (DDC, IMP)

Untitled.

PROJECT 10

VAN DYKE GARDENS 1974–75

All infrared 35mm negatives were made in 1974 and the prints were executed in 1974 and 1975. These photographs depict landscape views from Mexico and New Hampshire.

Van Dykes with applied watercolors.
12 1/2 x 18, 31.75 x 45.72
8 images made in Mexico; 8 made in New Hampshire
Printed on Rives, Arches Cover, and Arches Watercolor

PROJECT 11

PASSING SHOTS 1975–86

These are color (Ektacolor and Fujicolor) prints made from a Mick-A-Matic 126 cartridge toy camera. The camera was a gift to the artist from Phil Condax, curator of equipment at the George Eastman House in Rochester, New York. To date 144 negatives have been printed in this series of birds, flowers, fish, animals, and botanical gardens, and many have been printed more than once. The negatives were made in the United States, Spain, Portugal, Japan, and Australia.

Prints exist in three sizes: proof prints 8 x 8, 20.32 x 20.32; exhibition prints 15 1/4 x 15 1/4, 38.73 x 38.73; and a few are 20 x 20, 50.8 x 50.8. Additional printers include Christopher Grinnell and Scott Vlaun.

Titles:

1975

St. Petersburg, FL (elephant ear)
St. Petersburg, FL (flamingos) (JMSS, NASS)
St. Petersburg, FL (flamingo) (KF, NGC)
St. Petersburg, FL (cockatoo)
St. Petersburg, FL (swan tail)
St. Petersburg, FL (white bird)
St. Petersburg, FL (ostriches)
St. Petersburg, FL (school of fish)
St. Petersburg, FL (goldfish)
St. Petersburg, FL (flower)
St. Petersburg, FL (blue parrot)
St. Petersburg, FL (leaves)
St. Petersburg, FL (black swan)
St. Petersburg, FL (light and dark fish with palm)
St. Petersburg, FL (flower and river, v-shaped)
Tampa, FL (fish)

1976

Santa Rita, AZ (yucca) (JKJB)
Phoenix, AZ (fan leaf palm, lt.)
Phoenix, AZ (fan leaf palm)
Phoenix, AZ (fan leaf palm, dk.)
Tucson, AZ (lion)
Tubac, AZ (flowers)
Green Valley, AZ (arch)
Green Valley, AZ (penny)
Raleigh, NC (wing)
Valdosta, GA (sky)
Amarillo, TX (yellow curb)
Rochester, NY (flag)
Rochester, NY (flowers/shadows)
Rochester, NY (shadows)
Hollywood, CA (tree)
Buffalo, NY

San Diego, CA (parrot)
San Diego, CA (camel)
San Diego, CA (eagle head)
San Diego, CA (parrot feathers)
San Diego, CA (pink bird)
San Diego, CA (camel, large)
San Diego, CA (pink vegetation)
San Diego, CA (polar bear)
San Diego, CA (seed pod)
Maui, HI (palm tree)
Maui, HI (landscape) (UNM)
Maui, HI (Maui surf)
Maui, HI (rainbow) (KJV, UNM)
Maui, HI (beach view)
Maui, HI (view of surf)
Maui, HI (grass fire)
Culver City, CA (tite roof)
Culver City, CA (arch)
Culver City, CA (newspaper)
Long Beach, CA (Coppertone, head)
Long Beach, CA (Coppertone, torso)
Long Beach, CA (beach view)
Long Beach, CA (sun bathers)
Long Beach, CA (airplane)
Los Angeles, CA (ground cover)
Los Angeles, CA (sidewalk, flowers)
T or C, NM (ring bell)
T or C, NM (yellow building)
T or C, NM (blue chairs)
Socorro, NM (highway)
Albuquerque, NM (tree) (AM)
Albuquerque, NM (boot) (AM)
Albuquerque, NM (white horse head) (AM)
Albuquerque, NM (west mesa)
Albuquerque, NM (white horse shoulder)

1983

Arches, Garden of the Alcazer, Seville
Walkway, Garden of the Alcazar, Seville
Walls, Garden of the Alcazar, Seville
Foliage, Garden of the Alcazar, Seville
Palm Shadow, Garden of the Alcazar, Seville

Rochester, N. Y.

Gate, Garden of the Alcazar, Seville
Moorish Tiles, Garden of the Alcazar, Seville
Garden of the Alcazar, Seville
View of Intersection, Seville
Zigzag Path, Madrid Botanical Garden
Asters, Madrid
Flowers, Madrid Botanical Garden
Firecrackers, Madrid Botanical Garden
Peña Flor, Spain
Quintana del Puente, Spain
Outside Archena, Spain
View of Pond, La Alhambra, Granada
Fish Pond, La Alhambra, Granada
Shadows of the Alhambra Garden
Pond with Goldfish, La Alhambra
Lily Pond, La Alhambra
Pierced Ceiling, La Alhambra
Studio Window, Barcelona (ML, KJV)
Palm Leaves, Lisbon
Backlit Palm, Lisbon
Black and White Composition, Lisbon
Backlit Ferns, Lisbon
Banana Plant in Sunlight, Lisbon
Small Ferns, Lisbon
Palm, Lisbon

Flowers in Shadow, Lisbon
Fish Pond, Garden of Alhambra, Lisbon

1984

Plants, Kyoto Botanical Gardens
Plants in Pots, Kyoto, Japan
Specimen Plants, Kyoto Botanical Gardens (IJ, JBC)
Tree Azaleas, dark, Tokyo, Japan (ETB)
Tree Azaleas, Tokyo, Japan
View of Lily Pond, Tokyo, Japan
Hothouse Flowers, Kyoto Botanical Gardens,
    Kyoto, Japan
Greenhouse, Kyoto, Japan (IJ, EEO, NASS)
Greenhouse, Waterlilies #10, Kyoto, Japan
Greenhouse, Waterlilies #11, Kyoto, Japan
Greenhouse, Waterlilies #12, Kyoto, Japan
3 Koi, Yoyogi Park, Tokyo, Japan (DA, DCW)
Single Koi, Yoyogi Park, Tokyo, Japan
Koi in Sun, Yoyogi Park, Tokyo, Japan (HN, LC)
Curving Koi, Yoyogi Park, Tokyo, Japan
Pond at Shugakuin Palace, Kyoto, Japan (ETB)
Rock with Fallen Blossoms, Ryoangi, Kyoto,
    Japan (IJ, MR, MNM)
Koi Pair, Yoyogi Park, Tokyo, Japan (IJ, JR)
Path at Shugakuin Palace, Kyoto, Japan
Red Tulips, Kyoto Botanical Gardens, Kyoto, Japan
White Blossoms, Kyoto Botanical Gardens, Kyoto,
    Japan
Azaleas, Kyoto Botanical Gardens, Kyoto, Japan
Grass in Water, Tokyo, Japan

1986

Red Hibiscus, Sydney, Australia
Yellow Flower, Williams's Garden, Sydney, Australia
Williams's Garden, Sydney, Australia
Pink and Orange, Sydney, Australia
Pink Orchids, Sydney Botanical Garden, Sydney,
    Australia
Construction Barrier, Sydney, Australia
Clothespins, Sydney Backyard, Sydney, Australia
Kangaroo Paws, Perth, Australia (AN)
Azaleas, Part I, Perth, Australia
Azaleas, Part II, Perth, Australia

Azaleas, Part III, Perth, Australia
Stump with Pink Flowers, Perth, Australia
Wisteria, Quirindi, Australia
Wisteria 2, Quirindi, Australia
Wisteria 3, Quirindi, Australia
Fuschias and Chairs, Cairns, Australia
Fuschias, Cairns, Australia
Wildflowers, Ayers Rock, Australia
Painted Rose, Alice Springs, Australia
Soft Flower, Australia

Mega-chart.

PROJECT 12

COLORS PORTFOLIO 1975

These are offset lithographic prints. The first work contains nineteen portraits of the artist from her infancy to 1975, and the other four pieces are collage-like grids overlaid with images of irises. These were made exclusively for the *Colors* portfolio, a numbered edition portfolio conceived and directed by Robert

Fichter and funded by the National Endowment for the Arts and Florida State University Fine Arts Festival. Other artists who contributed to the portfolio were: Todd Walker, John Craig, Robert Heinecken, Darryl Curran, Henry Holmes Smith, Bea Nettles, Virgil Mirano, Eileen Cowin, and James Henkel.

20 x 24, 50.8 x 60.96
5 images
4 colors: cyan, magenta, yellow, black
Printed on Lancaster Bond by Rose Printing
Edition of 300

Titles:

Visual Autobiography (UNM)
Untitled #1 (UNM)
Untitled #2 (UNM)
Untitled #3 (UNM)
Untitled #4 (UNM)

Gift Horse.

PROJECT 13

MISCELLANEOUS HORSES 1978

The images used in these editions are circus publicity photographs that the artist found in an antique shop. One image shows the trick horse rider, Frances Kay

Haneford, in a handstand position on the back of a moving horse.

Trick Horse (MLS, YS)
Photo silkscreen
18 x 24, 45.72 x 60.96
1 color: gray with pink flocking
Printed on Rives
Edition of 25
Bon à tirer
4 color trial proofs
Unknown number of artist's proofs
Printed by Jim Kraft, Unified Arts, Albuquerque, New Mexico

Frances Kay Haneford
Van Dykes and cyanotyes with flocking
18 x 24, 45.72 x 60.96
Printed on Rives and Fabriano Classico
6 proof prints

Gift Horse (DO, JKJB, LA, NGC)
Photo silkscreen
21 x 25, 53.34 x 63.5
2 colors: brown, grey
Printed on Arches 88
Edition of 15
Bon à tirer
4 color trial proofs
Unknown number of artist's proof
Printed by Jim Kraft, Unified Arts, Albuquerque, New Mexico

PROJECT 14

CUT FLOWERS 1978–87

Cyanotypes, Van Dykes, monotypes, lithographs, photo silkscreens, and color photographs of still life flower arrangements made from 4 x 5 negatives with applied pastels, acrylic paints, watercolors, felt-tip markers, craypas, and metallic watercolors.

16 x 20, 40.64 x 50.8
Cyanotypes (CCP, HC, MC, NOM) (63)
Van Dykes (CCP, IN, MC, RES) (28)
Printed on Rives BFK, beige Rives, grey Rives BFK, Arches, buff Arches, Fabriano Classico, and Stonehenge
5 unique prints on Diazo paper
Color (Polacolor II) photographs 1979
24 x 20, 60.96 x 50.8

Titles:

White Chrysathemum X Changes
Cut Flowers: Roses (MNM, UAG) (3)
Cut Flowers: Delphiniums (UNM)
Cut Flower Variation
Cut Flower with Drawing
Hot Flower
Hot Flower Variation

Print editions:

White Chrysanthemum #1 1978–79 (CCP, RBG, SFM)
Lithograph with collotype transfer and applied ink
16 x 20, 40.64 x 50.8
4 colors: white, light grey, transparent silver, silver
Printed on gray Rives BFK
Edition of 20
Bon à tirer
2 trial proofs
13 color trial proofs
4 artist's proofs
2 Tamarind impressions
7 Roman-numbered editions
Printed by Conrad Schwable at Tamarind Institute, Albuquerque, New Mexico

Cut Flowers: 4 1979 (LU, MD, RBG)
Lithograph
16 x 20, 40.64 x 50.8
3 colors: brown, green, blue
Printed on white Arches
Edition of 10

Bon á tirer
1 trial proof
5 color trial proofs
2 artist's proofs
2 Tamarind impressions
7 Roman-numbered editions
Printed by Jeffrey Sippel at Tamarind Institute,
Albuquerque, New Mexico

Variation w/4 1979 (CC, MRU)
Lithograph
16 x 20, 40.64 x 50.8
3 colors: brown, pink, tan
Printed on white Arches
Edition of 10
Bon à tirer
1 color trial proof
2 Tamarind impressions
Printed by Jeffrey Sippel at Tamarind Institute,
Albuquerque, New Mexico

Cut Flowers: 6 1979 (RBG)
Lithograph
16 x 20, 40.64 x 50.8
5 colors: blue, pink, purple, gray, green
Printed on buff Arches
Edition of 10
Bon à tirer
7 color trial proofs
2 artist's proofs
2 Tamarind impressions
7 Roman-numbered editions
Printed by Bill Lagattuta at Tamarind Institue,
Albuquerque, New Mexico

Variation w/6 1979 (VDC)
Lithograph
16 x 20, 40.64 x 50.8
5 colors: dark blue, light pink, blue-green,
grey-green, green
Printed on buff Arches
Edition of 10
Bon à tirer

Iris Pair.

1 color trial proof
3 artist's proofs
2 Tamarind impressions
Printed by Bill Lagattuta at Tamarind Institue,
Albuquerque, New Mexico

Hot and Sour Flower x 4 1979 (JKJB, MLS, CCP,
JMSS)
Photo silkscreen with applied pastels
16 x 20, 40.64 x 50.8
3 colors: blue, green, pink
Printed on Arches 88
Edition of 27
Bon à tirer
3 color trial proofs
3 artist's proofs
Printed by Jim Kraft, Unified Arts, Albuquerque,
New Mexico

Amaryllis 1987 (CSF)
4 lithographic monotypes with cyanotype
19 1/2 x 23 1/2, 49.53 x 59.69

3 colors: blue, green, red
Sponsored by the College of Santa Fe
Printed by Hand Graphics, Santa Fe, New Mexico

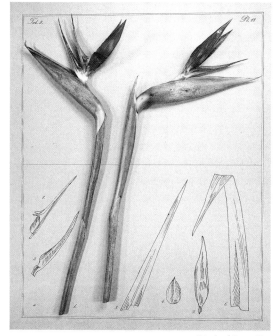

Bird of Paradise.

PROJECT 15

BOTANICAL LAYOUTS 1978–80, 1988

These are color (Polacolor II) photographs of still-life
flower arrangements in editions of 3 to editions of 40.

20 x 24, 50.8 x 60.96

Titles:

African Daisy 1979 (HM, NOM) (3)
Leaves 1979 (MNM) (5)
Peony I 1979 (4)
Peony II 1979 (CCP, DDM) (4)
Anemone 1980 (AS) (5)
Anemone Pavonina 1980 (AS, JBCC) (5)
Bird of Paradise 1980 (WLS) (5)

Calceolaria 1980 (AM) (5)
Tulip 1980 (PJS) (5)
African Daisy 1988 (AN) (5)
Carnation 1988 (PLB) (5)
Gladiola 1988 (EKCW) (5)
Stargazer Lily 1988 (EKCW) (5

Print editions:
Botanical Layout: Amaryllis Belladonna 1980
(LL, NOM, SFM)

This work was included in the portfolio "Five Still
Lifes" along with photographs by Robert Cumming,
Robert Fichter, Victor Schrager, and William Wegman.
The project was carried out at the Polaroid Corpora-
tion at the Massachusetts Institute of Technology in
Cambridge, Massachusetts.

20 x 24, 50.8 x 60.96
Edition of 40
10 artist's proofs
Published by Paradox Editions for Robert
Freidus Gallery, New York

Botanical Layout: Peony 1979 (AR, CCP, EEO,
KFK, LTB, MNM, PJS, WL)
Lithograph
22 x 18, 55. 88 x 45.72
5 colors: beige, yellow, green, brown, pink
Printed on white Arches
Edition of 40
Bon à tirer
11 color trial proofs
5 artist's proofs
1 presentation proof
2 Tamarind impressions
Printed by Jeffrey Sippel at Tamarind Institute,
Albuquerque, New Mexico

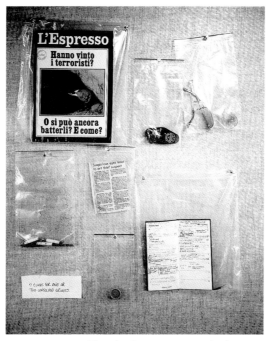

7 Clues for One or Two Unsolved Crimes.

PROJECT 16

MISCELLANEOUS POLAROIDS

These works are Polacolor II and black and white
Polaroid photographs.
20 x 24, 50.8 x 60.96

Inspired by the work of nineteenth-century American
trompe l'oeil painter John F. Peto (1854–1907), these
are still-life arrangements of memorabilia given to the
artist by her aunt and grandmother.

2 images

Titles:

Chicago Family: Aunt 1979 (HP, JKJB, MNM) (6)
Chicago Family: Grandmother 1979 (EEO, UNM) (6)

These are photographs of a collection of objects such
as a hotel key, a pair of broken eyeglasses, and an

appointment book, each in a plastic bag to simulate
police evidence.

2 images

Titles:

7 Clues for One or Two Unsolved Crimes 1980
(UNM) (3)
5 or 6 Clues Involving Contributory Negligence (3)

There is both a shift from black and white to color
and shift in the plane of focus in this sequence of a
still photograph and two women sharing a secret.

7 images

1 set of artist's proofs

Title:

Man Coming into Focus 1988 (4)

These are images of different sheets of origami paper
photographed against different color backgrounds.

5 images

Title:

A Japanese Collage in 5 Parts 1988 (3)

Individual still-life photographs of a gun, a Chinese
newspaper, and an embroidered silk purse.

3 images

Title:

Yin and Yang 1988 (3)

These images record the front and back of an
actual spy photograph of a camera.

2 images

Titles:

Teddy Bear (front) 1988 (3)
Teddy Bear (back) 1988 (3)

These images record the front and back covers of a Nazi propaganda book.

2 images

Titles:

In God's Own Land (front) 1988 (3)
In God's Own Land (back) 1988 (3)

Envelope from *Letter from the Chelsea Hotel*.

PROJECT 17

LETTER FROM THE CHELSEA HOTEL 1979 (JKJB)

The text is a letter written from the Chelsea Hotel in New York by Diana Luppi, a former student of Betty Hahn. Included with the portfolio is a 100% cotton T-shirt with a hand-screened image of the Chelsea Hotel letterhead. Additional T-shirts exist.

Photo silkscreen
30 1/4 x 21 1/4, 76.83 x 53.97
5 colors: blue, grey, black, tan, orange
Printed on Arches 88
Edition of 7
Bon à tirer
Each edition consists of 7 photo silkscreens, one T-shirt, and a portfolio case.
Printed by Jim Kraft, Unified Arts, Albuquerque, New Mexico

PROJECT 18

CRIME AND INTRIGUE SERIES 1979–82

Within each of these groups are color photographs, gelatin silver photographs, or lithographs made from 35mm negatives or transparencies.

Scenes of Crime 1979 (AP)
These images, made in Albuquerque, New Mexico, and on the island of Maui in Hawai'i, record simulated crime scenes that the artist constructed and then photographed.
Color (Ektacolor) photographs
8 x 10, 20.32 x 25.4
40 images
Only proof prints exist

A Case of XX (variant *A Case of Dos Equis*) 1981
This series shows thirty-three images of an apartment interior and exterior, Dos Equis beer bottle, and text borrowed from detective training manuals and mystery novels.
Gelatin silver photographs
1 set printed 11 x 14, 27.94 x 35.56
Selected images printed 18 x 24, 45.72 x 60.96
Additional images exist apart from the original thirty-three photographs

A Case of XX 1981 (CC, CCP, JKJB, MG)
Seven images from the original thirty-three, noted above, were printed in 1981 as a lithograph, with added red china crayon.

Photolithograph
20 x 24, 50.8 x 60.96
1 color: black
Printed on Arches
Edition of 27
Published and printed by the Minneapolis College of Art and Design, Minneapolis, Minnesota

Untitled, from *Scenes of Crime*.

Observations of British Intelligence 1981
This series made in London includes photographs of the façades of government buildings such as Whitehall, and interior views of underground tube stations. The artist followed a specific male figure throughout the city and recorded his daily activities.

Gelatin silver photographs
40 images—11 photographs of typed text; 29 photographs of city scenes
1 set of proof prints 8 x 10, 20.32 x 25.4
Projected exhibition print size 18 x 24, 45.72 x 60.96

Crime in the Home 1982
In this project there are eight photographs of household domestic items destroyed by the artist's Borzoi, Trotsky, when he was a puppy; one police sketch of the dog; and one image of the suspect's paws with a scale ruler.

Color (Cibachrome) photographs
11 x 14, 27.94 x 35.56
10 photographs
Edition of 3

Titles:

Crime in the Home 1982
Exhibit A: Oriental Rug Chewed
Exhibit B: Moccasin Attacked
Exhibit C: Second Oriental Rug Chewed

Exhibit D: Boot Toe Punctures
Exhibit E: Underwear, Molested
Exhibit F: Salt Shaker, Destroyed
Exhibit G: Cowboy Boot, Assaulted
Exhibit H: Cowboy Boot, Lighter, Assaulted
Exhibit I: Police Sketch of Subject
Exhibit J: Suspect in Fingerprint Lab

Ehrlichman Surveillance 1982
Gelatin silver photographs from 35mm negatives, mounted on foam core

These photographs were made at the Shidoni sculpture gardens and foundry in Tesuque, New Mexico, during a dinner held in honor of a group of visiting cultural attachés from the People's Republic of China. The white arrows in the photographs identify John Ehrlichman, former assistant of domestic affairs for Richard M. Nixon, and convicted felon who served eighteen months at the Federal Prison Camp at Safford, Arizona, for his role in the Watergate affair. Other guests included Bruce King, former governor, New Mexico; George Ewing, officer of cultural affairs for New Mexico; Ellen Bradbury, former director of the Museum of Fine Arts, Santa Fe; James Moore, director, Albuquerque Museum; Concha De Kleven, commissioner of fine arts, State of New Mexico; and Antoine Predock, architect.
16 x 24, 40.64 x 60.96
8 photographs in series
1 set of proof prints 11 x 14, 27.94 x 35.56

Project 19

Cinematic and Narrative Sequences 1984–87

All of these sequences are made from 35mm color and/or gelatin silver negatives, and some have added text.

Shinjuku 1984 (AM)
Color (Ektacolor) photographs from 35mm black and white and color negatives with white text composed by the artist. These photographs were made on two street corners in the Shinjuku district of Tokyo. This series was inspired by the transition of black and white to color imagery in the film version of *The Wizard of Oz*.

17 x 24, 43.18 x 60.96
11 photographs in series
Projected edition of 15
Printed by the artist and Hank Herrera

Appearance 1984 (ATAP)
These are gelatin silver photographs from 35mm negatives, mounted on foam core. This series records Clayton Moore during his personal appearance at the Queen of Heaven Catholic School in Albuquerque, New Mexico, in the summer of 1982. Moore was one of two actors who portrayed John Reid, "The Lone Ranger," in two feature films and the television series *The Lone Ranger* which began in 1949 and ran for eight years. The text was borrowed from *Wild Horse Canyon*, by Fran Stryker (New York: Grosset and Dunlap, 1950).

14 x 18, 35.56 x 45.72
22 photographs: 11 pairs of 1 each panel of text and 1 photograph
1 set of artist's proofs 11 x 14, 27.94 x 35.56

Fade to Black (Chinese) begun in 1985, work in progress
Color (Ektacolor) photographs from 35mm black and white and color negatives with white text. This sequence records the artist as she disappears into a crowd of people in Tiananmen Square, Beijing, China.

4 x 6, 10.16 x 15.24 and 8 x 10, 20.32 x 25.4
Only proof prints exist

Meditation, Identity, Proof 1986
Gelatin silver photographs from 35mm negatives. This sequence shows the progression of a hand moving toward an object on a desk top interspersed with a hand holding an ID photograph and a Japanese document.

Untitled, from *Meditation, Identity, Proof.*

18 x 24, 45.72 x 60.96
1 set of proof prints 11 x 14 (27.94 x 35.56)
7 images

Arrival or Departure (After Hitchcock) 1987
This series of gelatin silver photographs made from 35mm negatives shows sequential images of a man, Ira Jaffe, carrying luggage, and walking down the platform of the train station in Albuquerque, New Mexico. It was based on the opening scenes of Alfred Hitchcock's 1964 film *Marnie*.

17 x 24, 43.18 x 60.96
2 sets of proof prints 8 x 10, 20.32 x 25.4
5 images

Circumstances of Awakening; Berlin 1990 (LC, NS)
Color (Ektacolor) photographs from 35mm black and white and color negatives. These are color and gelatin silver filmstrip-like images that include a man asleep in a Berlin hotel room, a greenhouse, and a field of poppies.

19 x 24, 48.26 x 60.96
11 photographs in series
1 set of artist's proofs
Projected edition of 15
Printed by the artist and Christopher Grinnell

Circumstances of Transition, Berlin 1990
Color (Ektacolor) photographs from 35mm black and
white and color negatives that shows the reconstruc-
tion of the Brandenburg Gate in Berlin.

19 x 24, 48.26 x 60.96
5 photographs in series
1 set of artist's proofs
Edition of 5
Printed by the artist and Christopher Grinnell

Collect from Berlin 1991
These are photolithographs that were inspired by
grade B film noir movies.

27 x 36, 68.58 x 91.44
1 color: black
Printed on Lana Gravure
4 images in series
Edition of 11
1 set of artist's proofs
Printed by Rodney Hamon, Black and Blue Press,
Albuquerque, New Mexico

Titles:
Frame # 1 (MNM)
Frame # 2
Frame # 3
Frame # 4

PROJECT 20

AUSTRALIAN LANDSCAPES 1986–

These are color (Ektacolor) photographs from 35mm
negatives. They are film strip-like images that also
resemble the 1971 *Commemoratives* project.

16 x 20, 40.64 x 50.8 enlarged contact sheets from a
roll of 36 exposure film
Projected size 20 x 24, 50.8 x 60.96 enlarged contact
sheets
12 images to date; 6 made in Australia;
6 made at Mono Lake.

Australian Landscapes.

PROJECT 21

COLLOTYPE PROJECT 1987

This collaborative project was made possible through
a fellowship from the Visual Arts Research Institute at
Arizona State University at Tempe, and was produced
in its entirety in Tempe, Arizona.

Landscape with Cloud Variations 3.

Collotype with monotype
18 x 24, 45.72 x 60.96
2 colors: brown, blue
Printed on Arches 88
Edition of 10
Bon à tirer
2 printer's proofs
2 artist's proofs
11 Roman-numbered editions
Printed by the artist in collaboration with
Mark Klett, Jan Mehn, and Joseph Segura.

Titles:

Landscape with Cloud Variations 1
Landscape with Cloud Variations 2
Landscape with Cloud Variations 3
Landscape with Cloud Variations 4 (PTF)
Landscape with Cloud Variations 5

PROJECT 22

B WESTERNS 1991–

Monotypes with cyanotypes, Van Dykes, photolithographs, chine collé, and pencil. This group of prints
evolved from the *Lone Ranger* and *Landscape with
Cloud* series and was inspired by grade B Hollywood
westerns.

Sizes range from 19 1/2 x 27 1/2 to 25 1/2 x 36,
49.53 x 69.85 to 64.77 x 91.44
Printed on grey Rives and Fabriano Classico
3 dominant colors: white, brown, blue with
blended rolls
Only unique pieces
15 completed to date, 6 in progress
Printed by Rodney Hamon, Black and Blue Press,
Golden, New Mexico

"How Can You?"

PROJECT 23

SANTA FE MUSEUM PLATE PROJECT 1994

Bisque-fired and glazed ceramic dinner plates with a color lazer reproduction print of the Lone Ranger and Tonto laminated in the middle of each plate. Applied materials include silver stars and plastic silver toy bullets. This project was commissioned as a fund-raising

Taos Sky.

event by the Santa Fe Museum of Fine Arts, Santa Fe, New Mexico. Jenny Lind directed the project which included works by thirty-nine New Mexico artists.

11 inches in diameter, 27.94
14 plates in series
Plates are black and white and some have blue or variegated skies.

Titles:

Taos Sky (1)
New Mexico Sky (1)
Pecos Sky (1)
Starry Night (LCA, MNM) (6)
Untitled (FA) (5)

PROJECT 24

MISCELLANEOUS 1980–89

Art Removal Squad 1980
Two-sided instruction card composed of typed text and eleven illustrations—found drawings, comic strips, and various diagrams—printed in black on 8 1/2 x 11, 21.59 x 27.94 white card stock by a local copy store.

This work was requested by the editors of Blue Yonder Comic Books, Michael Reed and Jeff Bryan.

Equal Employment Opportunities for Women 1982
A sequence of four 11 x 14, 27.94 x 35.56 color (Ektacolor) photographs of the artist and Bruce King, former governor of New Mexico, made in the State Capitol building, Santa Fe, New Mexico.

Junior Prom Rephotographic Survey 1989
One gelatin silver photograph 5 x 7, 12.7 x 17.8 made 10 June 1956, and one 4 x 6, 10.2 x 15.2 color photograph made in June 1989. Both photographs were

taken by the artist's father in the Okon home at 152 North Franklin Road, Indianapolis, Indiana, and were processed and printed at a local drug store. Photographed with the artist is Jim Rupp.

Equal Employment Opportunities for Women.

COLLECTIONS

Abbreviations for collections precede each name and are cross-referenced with the individual works.

AAI	Akron Art Institute, Akron, Ohio
ACRA	A.C. & R. Advertising
ADE	Andy and Danica Eskind
AGV	Art Gallery, Vassar College, Poughkeepsie, New York
AI	Art Institute of Chicago, Chicago, Illinois
AK	Alan Klotz
AL	Mr. and Mrs. Arthur Lamb
ALH	Ann Lawhead
AM	Albuquerque Museum, Albuquerque, New Mexico
AN	Anne Noggle
ANB	Albuquerque National Bank, Albuquerque, New Mexico
ANE	Arnold Newman
AP	Antoine Predock
AR	Anthony Richardson
AS	Audrey Senturia
ATAP	Alex Traub/Andrea Poole
ATT	American Telephone and Telegraph Collection, New York, New York
AW	Ann Watson
BB	Babs Baker
BI	Barbara Ilardi
BL	Barbara London
BN	Bea Nettles
BNP	Bibliothèque Nationale, Paris, France
CAM	Crocker Art Museum, Sacramento, California
CAP	C & A Properties
CC	Carl Chiarenza
CCO	Cloritina Cocina

CCP	Center for Creative Photography, Tucson, Arizona
CJS	Carole and Jerry Sternstein
CM	Charlene McDermott
CMB	Chase Manhattan Bank, New York, New York
CMMP	Christopher Mead/Michele M. Penhall
CMP	California Museum of Photography, Riverside, California
CP	Capitol Records
CSF	College of Santa Fe, Santa Fe, New Mexico
CSUL	California State University Library, Long Beach, California
DAM	Denver Art Museum, Denver, Colorado
DB	Dan Berley
DCW	Deborah Cloud Waggoner
DDC	Darryl and Doris Curran
DDM	Donald and Donna McRae
DO	Dr. Diana Okon
DTC	Deutsche TeleCom Corporate Collection, Dusseldorf, Germany
EEO	Eugene and Esther Okon
EH	Eikoh Hosoe
EKCW	Emily Kass/Charles Weinraub
ENB	Exchange National Bank, Chicago, Illinois
ETB	Ed and Tamara Bryant
FA	Frank Aoi
FAM	Fogg Art Museum, Harvard University, Cambridge, Massachusetts
FBS	First Bank System, Minneapolis, Minnesota
FIC	Film-in-the-Cities, St. Paul, Minnesota
GA	Garo Antreasian
GB	Gus Blaisdell
GCG	Grunwald Center for the Graphic Arts, Los Angeles, California
GR	Gabriel T. Russo
GS	Georgia Smith
GW	Geoff Winningham
HC	Hallmark Collection, Kansas City, Kansas
HM	Houston Museum of Fine Arts, Houston, Texas
HN	Helen Nadler
HP	Hans Georg Puttnies

ICP	International Center of Photography, New York, New York
IJ	Ira Jaffe
IMP	International Museum of Photography at George Eastman House, Rochester, New York
IN	Ian North
IUAM	Indiana University Art Museum, Bloomington, Indiana
JB	James Borcoman
JBC	Jackie Chavez-Cunningham/Brad Cunningham
JC	JoAnn Callis
JES	Joel and Ellen Swartz
JF	Joan Fontcuberta
JG	Juliet Garza
JJB	J. J. Brookings Gallery
JJT	Joseph and Jean Tucker
JKJB	Jim Kraft/Judy Booth
JMSS	Judy Miller/Steve Stayton
JMY	Joan Myers
JP	John Pfahl
JR	James Rupp
JU	Jerry Uelsmann
JUP	John Upton
JV	JoAnn Verberg
KF	Karen Fabricius
KFK	Karl and Frances Koenig
KJV	Katherine and Jesus de Vilallonga
LA	Loretta Libby Atkins
LBC	Lincoln Bank Collection, Rochester, New York
LC	Louis Criss
LCA	Laura Carpenter
LL	Dr. Lester Lebo
LM	Louise Maffitt
LN	Lola Nirenberg
LP	Liverpool Museum, Liverpool, England
LTB	Laurie and Thomas Barrow
LU	Lehigh University Art Gallery, Bethlehem, Pennsylvania
MAC	Madison Art Center, Madison, Wisconsin
MB	Memphis Brooks Museum of Art, Memphis, Tennessee

MC	The Monsen Collection
MCA	Museum of Contemporary Art, Chicago, Illinois
MD	Marjorie Devon
MFA	Museum of Fine Arts, St. Petersburg, Florida
MG	Miguel Gandert
MI	Miho, Inc.
MIA	Minneapolis Institute of Arts, Minneapolis, Minnesota
ML	Marietta Leis
MLS	Margo Lynn Spiritus
MMA	Museum of Modern Art, New York, New York
MNM	Museum of Fine Arts, Museum of New Mexico, Santa Fe, New Mexico
MO	Mejo Okon
MR	Meridel Rubinstein
MRU	Marion Rush
NASS	Nick Abdalla/Susan Spring
NG	Northlight Gallery, Arizona State University, Tempe, Arizona
NGC	National Gallery of Canada, Ottawa
NJL	Nathan and Joan Lyons
NMAH	National Museum of American History, Washington, D.C.
NOM	New Orleans Museum of Art, New Orleans, Louisana
NS	Nadia Seluga
NSM	Norton Simon Museum, Pasadena, California
PAG	Picker Art Gallery, Colgate University, Hamilton, New York
PAM	Portland Art Museum, Portland, Oregon
PB	Peter Bunnell
PC	Polaroid Corporation Collection, Cambridge, Massachusetts
PJS	Patricia and Jerry Schoenfeld
PL	Patricia Lawhead
PLB	Paul and Lauren Bardacke
PLC	Paul and Lani Czyzewski
PN	Patrick Nagatani
PTF	Pritchard/Thorpe Family
RBG	Ray and Barbara Graham
RDG	Estate of Roberta De Golyer
RES	Richard and Elizabeth Santoro
RF	Robert Fichter
RH	Robert Heinecken
RJO	Reverend Jack Okon
RM	Roger Mertin
RMAC	Roswell Museum and Art Center, Roswell, New Mexico
RPI	Ryerson Polytechnic Institute, Toronto, Canada
RS	Estate of Rudolf Scopec
RSB	Robert A. Sobieszek
SAG	Sheldon Art Gallery, University of Nebraska, Lincoln, Nebraska
SC	Smith College Museum of Art, Northampton, Massachusetts
SD	Sally Dixon
SFM	San Francisco Museum of Modern Art, San Francisco, California
SH	Sandy Hume
SI	Smithsonian Institution, Washington, D.C.
SJU	San Jose State University, San Jose, California
SOR	Sophie Rivera
SPA	Spencer Museum of Art, University of Kansas, Lawrence, Kansas
SPB	Security Pacific Bank, Santa Ana, California
SR	Stuart Rome
TGM	The Green Museum, Osaka, Japan
UAG	University Art Gallery, New Mexico State University, Las Cruces, New Mexico
UC	University of Colorado, Denver, Colorado
ULPA	University of Louisville Photographic Archives, Louisville, Kentucky
UNM	University Art Museum, University of New Mexico, Albuquerque, New Mexico
UO	University of Oklahoma Museum of Art, Norman, Oklahoma
VDC	Van Deren Coke
VM	Virginia Museum of Fine Arts, Richmond, Virginia
VSW	Visual Studies Workshop, Rochester, New York
WAC	Walker Art Center, Liverpool, England
WAG	Wight Art Gallery, University of California, Los Angeles, California
WC	Williams College Museum of Art, Williamstown, Massachusetts
WL	Wayne R. Lazorik
WLS	Wanda Lee Smith
WT	William Tucker
YS	Yasu Suzuka

SELECTED EXHIBITION HISTORY

* Denotes a one-person exhibition

1966
"Seeing Photographically," International Museum of Photography at George Eastman House, Rochester, New York.

1967
"Photography Since 1950," organized by the International Museum of Photography at George Eastman House, Rochester, New York.

1968
"Two Photographers," with Gayle Smalley, Cabrillo College, Aptos, California.

1969
"Vision and Expression," International Museum of Photography at George Eastman House, Rochester, New York.
"Serial/Modular Imagery in Photography," Purdue University Fine Arts Gallery, West Lafayette, Indiana.
"The Photograph as Object," National Gallery of Canada, Ottawa.
"Women, Cameras, and Images II," with Gayle Smalley, Smithsonian Institution, Washington, D.C.

1970
"The Camera and the Human Facade," Smithsonian Institution, Washington, D.C.
"Applied Color," International Museum of Photography at George Eastman House, Rochester, New York.
"Into the 70's," Akron Art Institute, Akron, Ohio.
"Photography: New Acquisitions," Museum of Modern Art, New York, New York.

1971
* "Betty Hahn Photographs," Center for Photographic Studies, Louisville, Kentucky.
"Photography Invitational 1971," Arkansas Art Center, Little Rock, Arkansas, and Memphis Academy of Arts, Memphis, Tennessee.
"4th Annual International Miniature Print Competition and Exhibition," Associated American Artists Gallery, New York, New York.
"Contemporary Photographs," Museum of Modern Art, New York, New York.
"The Multiple Image," Massachusetts Institute of Technology, Cambridge, Massachusetts.

1972
"60's Continuum," International Museum of Photography at George Eastman House, Rochester, New York.
"Photography Invitational," Nova Scotia College of Art and Design, Halifax, Nova Scotia.
"The Market Diner Bash Group Show," The Underground Gallery, New York, New York.
"Photography Into Art," Camden Arts Centre, London, England.
"Historical Processes," Baltimore Art Museum, Baltimore, Maryland.
"The Multiple Image," Creative Photography Gallery, Massachusetts Institute for Technology, Cambridge, Massachusetts.

1973
"New Art from Photo-Sensitized Materials," Vassar College Art Gallery, Poughkeepsie, New York.
* "Betty Hahn—Photo Images," Riverside Studio, Rochester, New York.
"New Images 1839–1973," Smithsonian Institution, Washington, D.C.

"Light and Substance," University of New Mexico Art Museum, Albuquerque, New Mexico.
* "Betty Hahn," Witkin Gallery, New York, New York.
"Light and Lens," Hudson River Museum, Yonkers, New York.

1974
"New Images in Photography: Object and Illusion," Lowe Art Center, Coral Gables, Florida.
"Ladies' Choice," Fresno University Art Gallery, Fresno, California.
* "Betty Hahn—Stitched Gum Bichromate Prints," Focus Gallery, San Francisco, California.
"National Photography Invitational," Virginia Commonwealth University, Richmond, Virginia.

1975
"Women of Photography," San Francisco Museum of Modern Art, San Francisco, California.
"A Pictorial History of the World," Kansas City Art Institute, Kansas City, Missouri.
"East-West Trade Show," Portland Art Museum, Portland, Oregon.
"Photographs from the Collection," National Gallery of Canada, Ottawa.
"Sélections," Festival du Photographie, Arles, France.
"Women of Photography," Sidney Janis Gallery, New York, New York.

1976
"Photographic Process as Medium," Rutgers University Art Gallery, New Brunswick, New Jersey.
"American Family Portraits: 1730–1976," Philadelphia Museum of Art, Philadelphia, Pennsylvania.
"A Year's Acquisitions," Art Institute of Chicago, Chicago, Illinois.
* "Betty Hahn," Nexus Gallery, Atlanta, Georgia.
* "Betty Hahn: Passing Shots," New England School of Photography, Boston, Massachusetts.
* "Betty Hahn," The Silver Image Gallery, Tacoma, Washington.

1977

* "Betty Hahn: Color Photographs," Archetype Gallery, New Haven, Connecticut.
* "Betty Hahn," Sheldon Art Gallery, University of Nebraska, Lincoln, Nebraska.
* "Betty Hahn-Photographs," Southern Illinois University, Carbondale, Illinois.
"Untitled, 1st Photography Exhibition," Gallery Gemini, Palm Beach, Florida.
"Five Approaches to Color," The Santa Fe Gallery of Photography, Santa Fe, New Mexico.

1978

"Photography: New Mexico," American Cultural Center, Paris, France.
"23 Photographers/23 Directions," Walker Art Gallery, Liverpool, England.
* "Betty Hahn," Blue Sky Gallery, Portland, Oregon.
"Two from Albuquerque" (with Tom Barrow), Susan Spiritus Gallery, Newport Beach, California.
"Mirrors and Windows," Museum of Modern Art, New York, New York.

1979

* "Cut Flower Series," Witkin Gallery, New York, New York.
"Attitudes: Photography in the 1970's," Santa Barbara Museum of Art, Santa Barbara, California.
"Electroworks," International Museum of Photography at George Eastman House, Rochester, New York.
"20 x 24 Polaroid Color Photographs," Light Gallery, New York, New York.
"Art for the Vice President's Residence," Washington, D.C.

1980

* "Marked Photographs," Film-in-the-Cities, St. Paul, Minnesota.
* "Betty Hahn: 20 x 24 Polaroids," Wildine Gallery, Albuquerque, New Mexico.
"National Endowment for the Arts Purchase Award Artists," Center for Creative Photography, Tucson, Arizona.

"Five Still Lives," Robert Freidus Gallery, New York, New York.
"The Magical Eye: Definitions of Photography," National Gallery of Canada, Ottawa.

1981

* "Betty Hahn: 20 x 24 Photography," Fine Art Gallery, University of Colorado, Boulder, Colorado.
"Erweiterte Photographie," Fifth International Biennale, Wiener Secession, Vienna, Austria.
"A Decade of Collection: Master Photographs from St. Louis Private Collections," Gallery 210, University of Missouri, St. Louis, Missouri.
"Marked Photographs," Robert Samuel Gallery, New York, New York.
"The Manipulated Photo," Visual Arts Center of Alaska, Anchorage, Alaska.

1982

* "Betty Hahn: 20 x 24 Color Polaroids," Looking Glass Photography Gallery, Royal Oak, Michigan.
"Flowers," Witkin Gallery, New York, New York.
"The Alternative Image," Kohler Arts Center, Sheboygan, Wisconsin.
* "Betty Hahn," Columbia College Gallery, Chicago, Illinois.
* "Betty Hahn," Susan Spiritus Gallery, Newport Beach, California.

1983

"Women and Their Models," Catskill Center for Photography, Woodstock, New York.
"Printed by Women," Port of History Museum, Philadelphia, Pennsylvania.
"The Alternative Image," Toledo Museum of Art, Toledo, Ohio.
"Ten Photographers in New Mexico," Houston Center for Photography, Houston, Texas.
* "Betty Hahn," Moody Gallery of Art, University of Alabama, Tuscaloosa, Alabama.

1984

* "Betty Hahn," Port Washington Public Library, Port Washington, New York.

"Photographic Alternatives," Hong Kong Arts Centre, Pao Sui Loong Galleries, Hong Kong.
* "Betty Hahn," Louisiana Tech University, Ruston, Louisiana.
"Robert Mapplethorpe and Betty Hahn Photography," Carancahua Gallery, Corpus Christi, Texas.
* "Betty Hahn," Cameracases Gallery, University of Arkansas, Fayetteville, Arkansas.
* "Faculty Show—Betty Hahn," Art Museum, University of New Mexico, Albuquerque, New Mexico.
* "Betty Hahn," Clemson University Art Gallery, Clemson, South Carolina.

1985

"Hand Colored Photographs," Elaine Horwitch Gallery, Santa Fe, New Mexico.
"A Tribute to Lee D. Witkin," Witkin Gallery, New York, New York.
"Expanding the Perimeters of 20th-Century Photography," San Francisco Museum of Modern Art, San Francisco, California.
* "Passing Shots," Ruth Ramberg Gallery, Albuquerque, New Mexico.
"The American West: Visions and Revisions," Fort Wayne Museum of Art, Fort Wayne, Indiana.

1986

* Betty Hahn—Passing Shots," Georgia State University, Atlanta, Georgia.
* Betty Hahn—Alcove Show," Museum of Fine Arts, Museum of New Mexico, Santa Fe, New Mexico.
"Masterpieces from the Gallery Collection," Jane Corkin Gallery, Toronto, Canada.
"Artists in Mid-Career," San Francisco Museum of Modern Art, San Francisco, California.
* Betty Hahn—Non-Silver Prints," The Baker Gallery, Kansas City, Kansas.

1987

"Independent Associations: Robert Fichter, Betty Hahn, John Wood, Evon Streetman," Photographic Resource Center, Boston, Massachusetts.

"Working Small," Art Museum, University of New Mexico, Albuquerque, New Mexico.
"30 from 25," Sheppard Gallery, University of Nevada, Reno, Nevada.
"Photography and Art: Interactions since 1946," Los Angeles County Museum of Art, Los Angeles, California.

1988
* "Betty Hahn—Crime and Intrigue," Fort Wayne Museum of Art, Fort Wayne, Indiana.
"Reclaiming Paradise: American Women Photograph the Land," Tweed Museum, University of Minnesota, Duluth, Minnesota.
"Art Networks," Houston Fotofest, Houston, Texas.
"Passages in Time," Los Angeles Center for Photographic Studies, Los Angeles, California.
"Recent Trends in American Photography," Andrew Smith Gallery, Santa Fe, New Mexico.

1989
"The Second Ten Years," Witkin Gallery, New York, New York.
"The Modernist Still Life—Photographed," University of Missouri Art Gallery, St. Louis, Missouri.
"University of New Mexico Polaroid Shoot," Jane Baum Gallery, New York, New York.
"The Cherished Image: Portraits from 150 Years of Photography," National Gallery of Canada, Ottowa, Canada.
"Fantasies, Fables and Fabrications," Delaware Art Museum, Wilmington, Delaware.
* "Shinjuku," University Gallery, Fine Arts Center, University of Massachusetts.

1990
"Artists Who Love Nature: From Barbizon School to Contemporary Photographers," The Green Museum, Osaka, Japan.
"Art of Albuquerque," Albuquerque Museum, Albuquerque, New Mexico.
"The Collector's Eye," Museum of Fine Arts, Santa Fe, New Mexico.

"Fantasies, Fables and Fabrications," Phillips Exeter Academy Gallery, Andover, Massachusetts.
"Recent Collaborations," North Light Gallery, Arizona State University, Tempe, Arizona.

1991
* "Berlin Time Frames," Andrew Smith Gallery, Santa Fe, New Mexico.
"Photography from New Mexico," MOSFILM Studio Gallery, Moscow, Russia.
"Photography from New Mexico," Vision Gallery, San Francisco, California.
"Patterns of Influence," Center for Creative Photography, Tucson, Arizona.
"To Collect the Art of Women" and "The Jane Reese Williams Collection," Museum of New Mexico, Museum of Fine Arts, Santa Fe, New Mexico.

1992
"The Modernist Still Life Photographed," exhibition traveled to Pakistan, India, Saudi Arabia, Jordan, Egypt, Algeria, Morocco, and Greece.
"The Modernist Still Life Photographed," Center for Creative Photography, Tucson, Arizona.
"The View from Here: 75 Years at the Museum of Fine Arts"; "Artists of 20th-Century New Mexico: The Museum of Fine Arts Collection"; "New Mexico Impressions: Printmaking 1880–1990," Museum of Fine Arts, Museum of New Mexico, Santa Fe, New Mexico.

1993
"Flora Photographica: The Flower in Photography from 1835 to the Present," Vancouver Art Gallery, Vancouver, British Columbia.
"100th Birthday Anniversary Exhibition," Denver Art Museum, Denver, Colorado.
"New Acquisitions," Denver Art Museum, Denver, Colorado.
"Intentions and Techniques," Lehigh University Art Gallery, Bethlehem, Pennsylvania.
"New Mexico '93: Fine Arts, Fine Crafts," Museum of Fine Arts, Museum of New Mexico, Santa Fe, New Mexico.

"AIDS Benefit Exhibition," "Viva '93," Living Through Cancer Benefit Show, Kimo Art Gallery, Albuquerque, New Mexico.

1994
* "Passing Shots: A Travel Series by Betty Hahn," University of New Mexico Art Museum, Albuquerque, New Mexico.
"Flowers," Witkin Gallery, New York, New York.
"Paper Chase," Raw Space Gallery, Albuquerque, New Mexico.

1995
* "Betty Hahn: Photography or Maybe Not," a thirty-year retrospective organized by the Museum of Fine Arts, Santa Fe, New Mexico.

Contemporary Spanish Photography. Albuquerque: University of New Mexico Press, 1987.

"Henry Holmes Smith: Speaking with a Genuine Voice." *Image* 16, no. 4 (1973): 1–6.

"On Gum Bichromate Printing." In *Darkroom*, edited by Eleanor Lewis. New York: Lustrum Press, 1977.

"Women and their Models." *Center Quarterly* 4, no. 4 (1983): 4.

Abe, Yoshido, and Yasuo Murayama. *Artists Who Love Nature: From the Barbizon School to Contemporary Photographers*. Osaka: Green Museum, 1990.

Adams, Clinton. *Printmaking in New Mexico 1880–1990*. Albuquerque: University of New Mexico Press, 1991.

Albuquerque by Six [exhibition catalogue]. Essay by V. B. Price. Albuquerque: Albuquerque Museum, 1989.

"Anne Noggle, Betty Hahn." *Artweek* 4 (November 23, 1974): 11–12.

Asbury, Dana. "Mums and Kitsch." *Afterimage* (Summer 1979): 16.

———. "Large Scale Exuberance." *Artweek* (May 17, 1980): 16.

Barrow, Thomas. "On Betty Hahn." *Working Papers #1*. [St. Paul: Film-in-the-Cities] (November 1980).

Beerer, Pamela. "Innovative Photographer has First City Exhibition." *Albuquerque Journal*, April 27, 1980.

"Betty Hahn." *Artlines* 10 (October 1981): 13–15.

"Betty Okón-Hahn-Polka Z Chicago," *Panorama Polska-Nottingham* 18 (March 1994): 7.

Betty Hahn: Inside and Outside [exhibition catalogue]. Essay by Steve Yates. Bethlehem, Penn.: Lehigh University Art Galleries, 1988.

Bloom, John. "Interview with Betty Hahn." *Photo Metro* 51 (August 1987): 8–17, reprinted in *Photography at Bay: Interviews, Essays, and Reviews*, by John Bloom. Albuquerque: University of New Mexico Press, 1993.

Boyle, Marilyn. "4-Way Hotline to Reality." *Arizona Arts and Lifestyles* 4 (Winter 1981): 34–41.

Brodsky, Judith, and Ofelia Garcia. *Printed by Women*. Philadelphia: Print Club of Philadelphia, 1983.

Bunnell, Peter C. *Photographic Portraits* [exhibition catalogue]. Philadelphia: Moore College of Art, 1972.

Castellanos, Alejandro. "Fotografía Española (Contemporánea)". *Foto Zoom* 155 (August 1988): 16–22.

Champion, Tom, Robert Di Franco, and Christopher Rauschenberg, eds. *Blue Sky Gallery 1975–1980: Anniversary of an Alternative*. Portland: Blue Sky Gallery and Oregon Center of the Arts, 1980.

Donovan, Kevin. "Photography in New Mexico: The Graduate Program at the University of New Mexico, Albuquerque." *Creative Camera* 237 (September 1984): 1502–5.

Eden, Abby. "Betty Hahn." *Artspace* 2 (Winter 1976–77): 14–19.

Enyeart, James, ed. *Decade by Decade: Twentieth-Century American Photography*. Boston: Bullfinch Press/Little, Brown and Company, 1989.

198 Ewing, William A. *Flora Photographica: Masterpieces of Flower Photography 1835 to the Present*. New York: Simon and Schuster, 1991.

Fontcuberta, Joan. "La Camera Pobre." *PhotoVision* 17 (1986): 11.

"Gallery: Betty Hahn." *Art Express* 1 (May–June 1981): 50–51.

Gaston, Diana, "Passing Shots: A Travel Series by Betty Hahn" [exhibition brochure]. Albuquerque: University of New Mexico Art Museum, 1994.

Grundberg, Andy, and Kathleen McCarthy Gauss. *Photography and Art: Interactions Since 1946*. New York: Abbeville Press, 1987.

Hajicek James, and Margaret Moore, eds. *VARI Studios/ Northlight Gallery Recent Collaborations*. Tempe: Arizona State University, College of Fine Arts, 1990.

Hill, Brad. "Photo Artist-Betty Hahn." *Black and White* 9 (July 1980): 14–15.

Himelfarb, Harvey. *Forty American Photographers*. Sacramento: E. B. Crocker Art Gallery, 1978.

Hoy, Anne. *Fabrications*. New York: Abbeville Press, 1987.

Hume, Sandy, Ellen Manchester, and Gary Metz, eds. *The Great West: Real/Ideal*. Essays by Nathan Lyons and Gary Metz. Boulder: Department of Fine Arts, University of Colorado, 1977.

Johnston, Patricia. "Soft Images: Photography and Fiber Interact." *Views* 1 (1983): 9–12.

Kass, Emily. "An Interview with Betty Hahn." *Artspace* 3 (Summer 1985): 24–27.

Lloyd, Valerie. *23 Photographers/23 Directions*. London: Walker Art Gallery and the Arts Council of Great Britain, 1978.

Lyons, Nathan, ed. *Vision and Expression*. New York: Horizon Press and the George Eastman House, 1969.

———. *Photography in the Twentieth Century*. New York: Horizon Press, 1967.

McPhee, Laura. "On the Other-Hand." *Views* 3 (Spring 1987): 14.

Miho, James. "More than Real." *Communication Arts* 13, no. 6 (1972): 66–73.

Murray, Joan. "Seven Mid-Career Photographers." *Artweek* 23 (June 14, 1986): 11.

Moore, Sarah J. "Abstruse Dectective Stories." *Artweek* 30 (September 19, 1981): 11.

Parker, Bart, and Frank Martinelli. *The Multiple Image*. Kingston: University of Rhode Island Art Council, 1972.

Parker, Fred R. *Attitudes: Photography in the 70s*. Santa Barbara: Santa Barbara Museum of Art, 1979.

Putting the Pieces Together. Video produced by KNME, Albuquerque Public Television, 1992.

Scholl, Jane D. "Press the Button and Out Comes Art." *Smithsonian* 7 (October 1980): 26–27.

Schwable, Conrad, and John Sommers. "Betty Hahn's Lithographs." *The Tamarind Papers* 3, no. 2 [Albuquerque: Tamarind Institute] (1980).

Siegel, Judy. "Interview with Betty Hahn—Fusing Photo Processes, Painting and Technology." *Women Artists News* 7 (December 1979): 14–15.

Skarjune, David. "Betty Hahn Photographs: Hyperrealism or Illusion?" *Minnesota Daily*, November 21, 1980, 9 AE.

Sobieszek, Robert. "Chromzelationové Obrazy Betty Hahnové." *Czechoslovakia Photographie* 2 (1973): 62.

Spitzer, Neal. *New Art from Photosensitized Materials* [exhibition catalogue]. Poughkeepsie: Vassar College Art Gallery, 1973.

Stranieri, Autori. "Betty Hahn." *Progresso Fotografico* 3 (March 1980): 48–49.

Szarkowski, John. *New Images in Photography: Object and Illusion* [exhibition catalogue]. Coral Gables: University of Miami Lowe Art Museum, 1974.

Theil, Linda. "Photoprocess." *Flying Needle* 2 (May 1981): 20–21.

Tucker, Jean S. *Aspects of American Photography*. St. Louis: University of Missouri, 1976.

———. *The Modernist Still Life—Photographed*. St. Louis: University of Missouri Office of Publications, 1989.

Vandersteel, Dorothy. *Artists in Mid-Career* [exhibition catalogue]. San Francisco: San Francisco Museum of Modern Art, 1986.

Women of Photography: An Historical Survey [exhibition catalogue]. Essays by Margery Mann and Anne Noggle. San Francisco: San Francisco Museum of Modern Art, 1975.

Zelich, Cristina. "Los Fotógrafos/The Photographers." *PhotoVision* 10 (1981): 8.

BETTY HAHN: PHOTOGRAPHY OR MAYBE NOT

Edited by Dana Asbury

*Composed in Sabon with Galliard display using
Quark XPress, version 3.3 for Windows*

*Text film output by Integrated Composition Systems,
Spokane, Washington*

*Color separations, printing, and binding
by Sung-In Printing America, Inc.*

Text printed on 150 gsm Velvet Art

*Designed by Kristina Kachele in
collaboration with Betty Hahn*

Printed in Korea